Weeping Violins

Weeping Violins

THE GYPSY TRAGEDY IN EUROPE

BETTY ALT &
SILVIA FOLTS

THOMAS JEFFERSON UNIVERSITY PRESS
KIRKSVILLE, MISSOURI
1996

MAR 10 '97 940.53/8
Ael 79 w)

Copyright © 1996 by Thomas Jefferson University Press
at Truman State University
Kirksville, Missouri, 63501-4221 USA

Distributed by arrangement with
University Publishing Associates, Inc.
4720 Boston Way, Lanham, Maryland 20706

3 Henrietta Street, London WC2E 8LU England

British Cataloging in Publication information available.

Library of Congress Cataloging -in-Publication Data
Alt, Betty Sowers.
    Weeping violins : the Gypsy tragedy in Europe / Betty Alt and Silvia Folts.
    p.   cm.
    Includes bibliographical references and index.
    ISBN 0-943549-31-0 (case)   0-943549-39-6 (paper)
    1. Gypsies—Europe. 2. Europe—Ethnic relations. 3. World War, 1939–1945—
Gypsies—Europe. 4. World War, 1939-1945—Atrocities. I. Folts, Silvia, 1953- . II.
Title.
IN PROCESS
940.53'18—dc20   95-25989
                                                                CIP

∞ The paper used in this publication meets the minimum requirements of the American National Standard for Permanence of Paper for Printed Library Materials ANSI Z39.48, 1984.

For David, Patrick, Bill, and Eden,
and for Peter Rose

Contents

Contents

Preface

∾

The most urgent research now needed is oral history *with Gypsy survi-vors [of the holocaust].*

—Gabrielle Tyrnauer, 1989

CERTAINLY, THE AUTHORS CONCUR with Gabrielle Tyrnauer. Too few Gypsy survivors of the holocaust are alive today. Of those who are, some are reluctant to provide documentation as it forces them to relive and to be haunted by the painful memories of countless days of horror. The wife of one survivor said, "After my husband has talked with you, it is as certain as the sun rises in the morning that he will have bad dreams for several nights afterwards. He will awaken sweating, gasping, reliving those days of hell."

Other Gypsy survivors were cautious about being interviewed and wished to retain their anonymity, fearful that the centuries-old prejudices against all Gypsies will affect their children and grandchildren today. For-tunately, several survivors were willing and anxious to tell their stories because they felt their tragedy had been ignored by the world

However, the havoc that cost the lives of so many Gypsies in the death camps of the Third Reich cannot be fully understood without an examination of the centuries of European persecution which paved the way for anti-Gypsy laws, discrimination, and death. Only recently has there been much work on Gypsy history, and, other than the 1976 book by Donald Kenrick and Gratton Puxon, little attention has been given in the United States to the holocaust period as it affected Europe's Gypsy popula-tion.

While the authors are aware that millions of men, women, and chil-dren from various racial, ethnic, and religious backgrounds perished during the Nazi regime, this book is solely concerned with the reasons behind the mass murder of the Gypsies, the stories of some of the Romany survivors, and the continuing persecution of this minority. Silvia Folts, herself the daughter of a Gypsy survivor of Auschwitz, and Betty Alt hope that this overview will help to fill the existing gap in Gypsy history and bring to the public's attention the nearly forgotten tragedy that was perpetrated upon these "stepchildren" of society.

The authors wish to thank all of those individuals who were willing to be interviewed or who so generously shared information, especially Dr. Ian Hancock. Thanks is also given to members of their families for their patience and support.

One

∾

Centuries of Persecution

*...but who speaks of the tragedy of the Gypsies, who knows that over a
million Gypsies without a doubt perished in the extermination camps?
And the Nazis would have gassed six million if the Gypsies had been as
numerous [as the Jews].*
— Simon Wiesenthal, 1989

WE WERE UNLOADED FROM the transport at Platerowa and put into a one-room schoolhouse. We all were beaten with whips, even my little sisters and brothers." Beneath their typed sterility, these words in the German court records fail to portray the years of fear and horror. "We had to lie on the floor. We had no blankets, nothing. We were not allowed to take anything on the transport. Around the schoolroom lay strewn partially decomposed corpses of Polish soldiers and horse carcasses. We got no water. My mother gave us urine to drink."

Thus, in 1940, did Wanda G., a German Sinti Gypsy, begin five years of holocaust survival. Although most of Wanda's extended family either died of disease or was gassed in the Third Reich's concentration camps, Wanda survived—mutilated and disabled, but alive. Her roundup and incarceration were merely a harbinger of what would happen to hundreds of thousands of European Gypsy families during World War II. However, this sort of treatment was not unusual; it was typical of what Gypsies have endured for many centuries. In practically all countries, the Gypsies have been unwelcome wanderers. Even when they gave up their nomadic lifestyle and established homes and businesses, seldom did they become an integrated part of their host society. Rumors abounded about their origin and the reason for their endless wandering.

CHAPTER ONE

ORIGIN AND MIGRATION

Certainly there are many fascinating explanations about the origins of the dark-haired, dark-skinned travelers who appeared in Eastern Europe in the tenth century. One legend tells that the Gypsies were descendants of Adam and a woman created before Eve. Another proposed that they were descendants of a prehistoric people who had been roaming the world for eons. Another said they were related to people who lived in the Caucasus. Still others felt they were akin to the Jews, the Moors, the Nubians.[1]

Some sources speculate that the Gypsy originally migrated from Egypt (hence the name Gypsy from the "gyp" in Egypt). The Egyptian connection was strengthened by those who said that Gypsies had fled from Egypt with Joseph and Mary[2] while those arriving in Scotland in 1505 told that their leader was lord of "little Egypt." In 1514, a Gypsy palmist was described as an "Egyptian" woman who could tell of marvelous things. Early Gypsies arriving in Western Europe possibly presented themselves as pilgrims traveling from "little Egypt," which may have been merely another name for the Middle East.[3] Around 1610 a pamphlet described them as going "alwais never under an hundred men or women, causing their faces to be made blacke, as if they were Egyptians."[4] While all of these legends, rumors, and innuendos are intriguing, there is almost no proof available to support the Egyptian origin.

Today, most scholars agree that the Gypsies originated in India and left that land about 1,000 years ago. (However, a Persian poet mentions a nomadic group of 10,000 Luri musicians in 420 B.C., which may be the earliest reference to Gypsies found so far.)[5] Perhaps they are descendants of the Sansi, a nomadic group who still live near Delph, India. On the other hand a 1922 linguistic study by Sir George Grierson links the European Gypsy to tribes in the extreme northwest of India, particularly the Dom. Some scholars believe the word *Rom* (short for Romany, used by many to refer to the Gypsy language and various clans, particularly those who continue a nomadic existence) comes from the word *Dom*. Or there are the Banjaras, who are found across much of India and who, like Europe's Gypsy population, were wanderers.[6]

Their true origin is further complicated by the fact that as they wandered, the Gypsies became known by different names in different countries. They were Bohemians in France, Tartars in Germany, Heathens in the

Netherlands, and Athingani in Greece. Hungarians many times referred to them as "Pharoah's people"; the English called them Egyptians. The German term *Zigeuner* (used throughout this book) is derived from the German *ziehender Gauner,** which is translated by some to mean "nomadic rascal." The Gypsies call themselves *Rom*, which in their language originally meant "a man of our own race."[7]

Why the Gypsies began their endless migration across the Asian and European continents remains as much a mystery as their origin. If they were originally Banjaras, a ruling Indian class that supposedly provided warriors for Alexander the Great,[8] changes in government or economic misfortune may have caused them to become wanderers. Another legend says their wandering is punishment for their refusal to give sanctuary to the Holy Family during its sojourn in Egypt.[9] A Gypsy woman interviewed in 1991 gave an even more interesting explanation. "We are being punished for stealing the fourth nail that was needed in Christ's crucifixion. That is why his feet are crossed and nailed together. There was a nail for each hand and one for each foot. Our wandering is punishment for taking the fourth nail. I remember hearing this as a child in Europe."

Regardless of why they took up the nomadic lifestyle, by the time the Gypsies reached the European continent, most land was already owned by other races and ethnic groups who were definitely unwilling to share it. This made it difficult for the wanderers to establish permanent settlements, although a few were able to do so. A permanent Gypsy village existed in the Balkans in 1378, and nearly a hundred years later travelers mention a settlement of three hundred Gypsy families in Greece.[10] In Western Europe a lighter-skinned group known as the Sinti (Sinte) were tolerated as migratory workers and, eventually, were partially integrated into the various European cultures.

However, in general the nomadic Rom eluded assimilation. Most found a livelihood on the edge of established society—roaming from village to village, living off the land, stereotyped as second-class people and viewed with prejudice and suspicion. Always a minority, they easily became prey to "scapegoating." Persecution was expected and quickly became a way of life. If something was missing, the Gypsies had taken it. If some evil befell a

*Other meanings for *Gauner* are: swindler, cheat, trickster.

town, the Gypsies had caused it. Punishment was many times harsh and ran the gamut from slavery to death.

CONTINUOUS OPPRESSION

Although the issue of slavery is still disputed by some historians, for many Gypsies it appears that slavery became a way of life, at least during the early centuries of their migration across Europe. Some writers believe that the Gypsies were slaves from the time of their arrival in the southeastern part of the continent. Documents allude to Gypsy slavery in the Balkans as early as 1348. While the figures may be exaggerated, a record from 1471 states:

> [T]he Moldavian prince, Stephan the Great, after a victorious war with his Wallachian neighbors, transported into Moldavia 17,000 Tsigani in order to use their labour force.[11]

In the Rumanian principalities from the fourteenth century until 1856, Gypsies became slaves of the state, the clergy, or the nobility. For example, Rumanian Civil Code placed the Gypsy into a virtual caste system, specifying that every Gypsy was automatically born a slave and that the children of a Gypsy slave also were slaves. In addition to the Gypsies' freedom being taken away, their masters had the right to inflict severe punishment. Some were badly beaten; some were hung over smoke, chained hand and foot, or thrown naked into snow. Newspapers carried announcements of public sales of Gypsy slaves, and many families were torn apart.[12]

Not only were enslaved Gypsies punished; the mere fact that one had Gypsy blood was reason enough for the authorities to inflict various forms of torture. In Germany in the 1700s a sign showing a Gypsy on his way to the gallows, his flesh whipped from his body, states: "Punishment for Gypsies and their women found in this country." In Prague, which earlier had been somewhat tolerant of Gypsies, Joseph I issued an edict stating that all Gypsy men be hanged without trial and that Gypsy boys and women be mutilated.[13] Charles VI passed a law that any male Gypsy found in the country was to be killed instantly. In 1826, a German named Freiherr von Lenchen publicly displayed the severed heads of a Gypsy woman and her child, his trophies from the sport of Gypsy hunting. Gypsy hunts were also popular in Switzerland, Germany, and the Netherlands.[14]

To prevent the Gypsies' continual wandering, prohibitions against nomadism were put into effect in almost every European country at some time, beginning with Spain in 1492. The Spanish decree ordered that Gypsies must cease traveling together within sixty days. Failure to comply could result in severe punishment such as:

> ...100 lashes and banishment. For repeat offenders, amputation of ears, 60 days in chains and banishment. Third-time offenders to become slaves of those who captured them.[15]

Maria Theresa of Austria and her successor, Joseph II, tried to get Gypsies to settle down as farmers and assimilate into Austrian society. To accomplish this assimilation, Gypsy clothing and music were prohibited. A punishment of twenty-five lashes could be administered to Gypsies who were caught speaking their native Romany. Intermarriage with non-Gypsies was forbidden, a practice which did nothing to hasten integration during the settlement process.[16] As can be seen, documenting the oppression is easy; explaining the reasons for it is more difficult.

Once a Gypsy, Always a Gypsy

In the 1400s a few European regions, such as Slovakia, had tentatively put out a "welcome mat" for Gypsies. King Matthias and King Vladislav, as well as several other kings, wrote letters of commendation and safe conduct orders for Gypsies. Prague officials allowed Gypsies to stay in that town in 1523, and during this time period several Slovakian towns presented gifts to the nomadic clans.[17] However, these actions were certainly the exception rather than the rule. The incidents of welcome were temporary at best, and integration into Western society was definitely discouraged.

To begin with, for many Europeans, and even in Asia where lighter-colored skins were preferred, the Gypsies' dark skin made them objects of ridicule, . The Persian poet Firdausi is said to have written, "No washing ever whitens the black Gypsy." A German monk in the city of Lübeck described Gypsies he had seen as having the "most ugly faces, black like those of Tartars," while an old Russian Yiddish proverb stated, "The same sun makes the linen white and the Gypsy black."[18] When Gypsies arrived at the gates of Paris, a French author described the men as "...very dark and their hair was crisp; the women were the ugliest and swarthiest one could see; their faces were all lined and their hair was as black as a horse's tail...."[19] Also, many Northerners considered the Gypsies' darker skin to be symbolic of evil. Except along the Mediterranean where the pigmentation of most residents tended to be of a brown hue, the Gypsies' dark coloring quickly set them apart from the lighter pigmentation of the Northern European population and made them easily recognizable prey for prejudice and discrimination. Even if the Gypsy had wished to assimilate, his skin color hindered him from doing so.

Earning a living also caused friction between the Gypsies and their hosts. Without land for farming, both the sedentary Gypsies and the Rom had to find other means of support. Whether settled or migrant, as the Gypsies became a part of the labor market, they created an additional labor force. Most times this placed a burden on the local economies, which were hard pressed to absorb the additional workers. Some Gypsies earned money through what were considered "Gypsy skills," such as music and dancing; others performed in or trained animals for the circus. In addition, however, Gypsies were involved in blacksmithing, basket weaving, shoe making, and metalworking—trades of the non-Gypsy guild members. Since some of the Rom handiwork proved superior to that of the local craftsmen, Gypsies found themselves in direct competition with guild members. The guild masters and their apprentices were not tolerant of this competition from what they saw as wandering vagrants. They were unwilling to accept Gypsies into the guilds, and left the wanderers with little access to many jobs.

Other economic pressures were also applied. Portugal forbade Gypsies to purchase houses in the mid-1600s. During the same century, Gypsies were barred by law in Serbia from manufacturing copper utensils. In Hungary the Guild of Locksmiths successfully kept Gypsies from doing any metalworking *outside* their tents, where they could display their wares to shoppers. In mid-eighteenth-century Russia, extra taxes were levied on Gypsies. An Albanian law barred Gypsies from earning money by dancing in public, and eventually they had to pay a special fee to license performances.[20] With the difficulties involved in earning a living in a settled community, it is no wonder the Gypsies continued to roam the countryside and live off the land.

To survive, some Gypsies turned to begging, stealing, and pilfering as they roamed the countryside. It was only a matter of time until the authorities throughout Europe received complaints about the "bad qualities" of the Gypsies and the trouble and disturbances they were causing. From Portugal to Scandinavia they were accused of many crimes, even though it was probably only a small percentage of their people who were actually involved.[21]

Less than fifty years after the first Gypsies had entered Western Europe, complaints reached the authorities about their bad qualities, their small-scale thefts, and the "trouble, damage, and many disturbances" they brought with them. In the mid-1500s a French lawyer justified expulsion of the Gypsies from France on similar grounds:

> It was very necessary to remove these terrible persons from the simple common people on whom they had played a thousand tricks and subtle swindles, claiming that they...foretell life and death, conspired to give young people love potions and drugs...and never left a place without having evilly stolen something.[22]

The question of thievery as a Gypsy characteristic has been hotly debated. Many Gypsies admit that there was occasional theft. Supposedly towns contained areas of "good" Gypsies, those who did not steal, and "the others," thieves and pickpockets. One early Persian poet may have contributed to this stigma of "thief." He tells of a shah who sent word to India requesting harpists and was sent Indian Gypsies, "Luris...riding on ducks—a joking reference to that tribe's known love for stealing fowl."[23]

On the other hand, some Gypsies explain that there is a necessity for "subsistence thieving" but that this theft has been greatly exaggerated. Since they are constantly mobile, when they need hay for their horses, firewood, some garden vegetables, or a "stray" chicken, "they consider the entire Gaje (non-Gypsy) world a public domain.... If they were guilty of all the thefts blamed on them, they would have to travel with moving vans or settle down under the weight of their possessions."[24]

For others, and again this became a stereotype for all, begging was a chief means of support. "Mong, chavo, mong!"*—Romany for "Beg, boy,

---

*Mong, according to some Gypsies does not always mean to beg. Many Gypsies would sell items like buttons, zippers, combs, safety pins, shoelaces, and so forth, from door to door. They would then say, "We go mongen."

beg"—were the words one mother used as she taught her son how to beg from the non-Gypsies.[25] Perhaps, as one source suggests, the constant begging of many of the women and children was a way of getting what they needed and yet discouraged lengthy contact between Gypsies and the Gaje. Nevertheless, the labels of thief and beggar were always with them (and continue to be so today).

Not only were they accused of day-to-day crimes, but a hint of guilt was attached to being Gypsy which did not endear them to those who espoused Christian doctrine. Supposedly, as a Spanish carol suggests, Gypsies stole Jesus' swaddling clothes from the manger. Some said the Gypsies had denied shelter to Mary and Joseph; others felt that, along with the Jews, the Gypsies shared some of the blame for the death of Christ.[26] With these accusations being bandied about, it was only a matter of time before the Church would become involved with the "Gypsy problem."

The Church did little to suppress the accusations against the Gypsies and, in general, supported anti-Gypsy laws. As early as 1560 the archbishop of Upsala, Sweden, had published a decree which stated that "no priest shall have any intercourse with the Gypsies, nor bury their dead, nor baptize their children."[27]

In 1568, Pope Pius V attempted to expel all Gypsies "from the domain of the Roman Catholic Church."[28] Two men were fined by the presbyters of Aberdeen, Scotland, for selling meat and drink to Gypsies. Pope Pius V expelled from Rome a monk who dared oppose his order that male Gypsies "be sent to the galleys to serve at the battle of Lepanto." Protestant clergy shared the antagonism of their Catholic brothers. A Lithuanian minister stated that "Gypsies in a well-ordered state are like vermin on an animal's body."[29]

It would not be until the nineteenth century that the Church would begin to take a more benevolent interest in Gypsies. In the 1800s missions and schools were founded for Gypsies in England, Germany, Italy, Belgium, and Spain.[30] Still, few of the clans came into contact with these church efforts, possibly because of distrust, disinterest, or the Gypsies' highly mobile lifestyle. When Gypsies did convert to Christianity (and most of them eventually embraced Catholicism), the Church tended to feel that many of them had done this solely for the purpose of gaining special favors or rewards. In addition, the belief in and practice of sorcery and witchcraft by some Gypsies would further alienate them from the Christian Church and their host societies.

Possibly one of the chief Gypsy activities which antagonized the Church and a good portion of the general populace was fortune-telling. Although, as most sources agree, Gypsy women probably began telling fortunes as a way to get money from the Gaje, this activity created around them a mystical aura. Again legends were created. Gypsies had magic powers; Gypsies could foretell the future; Gypsies could cast spells.

Gypsy predictions for the future and magic practices held a strong attraction for Europe's uneducated populace. At times these feats came into open competition with the claims in the sphere of the supernatural made by the priests, and the Church retaliated against its members who sought Gypsy advice. At one time the bishop of Paris excommunicated those people whose palms had been read by Gypsies. The French ecclesiastical court at Troyes ordered parishioners to offer candles as a penance for having had their palms read.[31] (Generally speaking, little encouragement was offered for Gypsies to become members of the Church and give up their heathen practices.)

Of course, the Gypsies were quick to take advantage of the Gaje's belief in their legendary powers and their use of the evil eye. If a plea to "cross my palm with silver" failed to get results, an implied threat of a spell of bad luck would usually get the desired outcome. An old Gypsy woman who lived in a settled village near Belgrade, Serbia, in the late 1980s, and who learned the art of fortune-telling and magic from her mother explained:

> If a man is sick, I act upon the sickness.... If he's unhappy, I work on bringing back his happiness. I make him a talisman—not the kind worn from birth to protect the child from evil spirits, but the other kind, made according to need. The kind of talisman I make, the wing of a bat or suchlike is placed under the pillow.... It sees in the dark, so it can find and return lost happiness.... Not everybody can put a bat-wing under the pillow for it to work. It can be done only by someone who communes with the spirit world—I can do it...other Gypsy women in the place cannot.[32]

9

While the Gypsies may not have believed in their own powers of fortune-telling, an uneducated European population was both fascinated and frightened by these supposed skills. For centuries, government authorities and the church continued to rail against the practice of fortune-telling, but with little results.

Another reason for the Gypsies' continued persecution may have been a result of their strong ties to those people of their own blood and language rather than to the people of the societies in which they camped or took up semipermanent residence. Family and tribal commitments were always extremely important. Marriages were to be endogamous (marriage within the clan), a practice still favored by many Gypsies today. One Gypsy interviewed recalled how, in the mid-1970s a woman married a non-Gypsy, a medical doctor. For this indiscretion, she and her family were considered as being outside the Gypsy family group. It was explained that the practice of medicine is considered by some "to be against the law, like eating pork for Jews. It disturbs the dead." While the Gypsies were to a large extent economically dependent on the Gaje, they definitely did not wish to intermarry or adopt Gaje culture.

On the whole Gypsies were suspicious of friendships with the Gaje, even if these outsiders had wished to infiltrate or to learn more about the Gypsy subculture. In addition, Gypsies discouraged teaching outsiders the Romany language, a feat which would have been difficult anyway, since Romany was only a spoken language until the latter part of the twentieth century, when it was finally put into written form.

Because of the exclusivity brought about by communication barriers and the autonomy of the clans, the Gypsies were little concerned with the Gaje world. Their authority was that of the tribal group. As they saw it, Gaje laws were meant solely for the non-Gypsy. Had they integrated into the dominant culture, the Gypsies would have essentially lost their language, customs, and characteristics—their unique identity. They chose to remain as separate as possible from the Gaje, a separateness which the established people in the various European countries found unacceptable. Some may even have felt the Gypsies' seclusion to be a threat. Therefore, it was not difficult for those who were dominant to justify and continue oppressive measures against a group which actively avoided accepting or conforming to the norms of European society.

Modern Times

As the twentieth century began and the world moved into "modern times," many of the Rom were still considered "stateless" people, carrying only temporary identification papers. Supposedly, they were allowed to pass through one country only on their way to the next one; they were not allowed to loiter. As they migrated, different arrangements had to be made regarding their status. "In France there was the much hated and oppressive institution of the *Carnet Anthropometrique*, one of the most discriminatory permits of residence, requiring registration *every twenty-four hours* at the local police headquarters."[33] Because of this type of restriction, many Gypsies would give up their roaming and try to settle into the urban life of Europe.

Shortly after the First World War, some countries in Eastern Europe had attempted to fit the Gypsies into a sedentary lifestyle. In Czechoslovakia, a special open-air school, surrounded by trees and a playground, was started for Gypsy children. Since the curriculum included drawing, handicrafts, and violin instruction, the institution became a general cultural center for the Gypsies in that area. There were also Romany newspapers in Romania, Yugoslavia, and the Soviet Union, and a few Gypsy professional people were making an appearance on the European scene.[34] These progressive measures were the exception rather than the rule, however. Most countries still followed a policy of repression and/or persecution of the Gypsies, particularly the nomadic Rom.

Unlike the Rom, the Sinti Gypsies gathered in the large cities of the industrialized European nations of Western Europe and accepted a settled existence. Having lived for several generations in the same locale, they tended to become a part of the local labor force; some even opened small businesses of their own. To some degree the Sinti were tolerated by the dominant society. Yet the Gaje's suspicion and dislike of anyone with Gypsy blood would merely lie hidden and resurface at a later time.

Because of the discrimination against those who continued their nomadic ways, the family of Pollo R. had elected to settle down. Most times this called for a drastic change in lifestyle. Pollo recalled at age sixty how he felt as a small boy when his family exchanged their horses and wagon for a permanent residence:

Although I was only four years old at the time, I remember being quite unhappy when we took leave from Max, the horse. Things changed dramatically for me; no more sitting around the fire in the evening; no more going to the Rhine river with the horses. My brothers Wunderli and Thomas would take me along to the river, where we would first wash the horses. Afterwards they would put me atop Lucia's (the horse's) back, and she would swim with me around the river. We had neither a care in the world, nor the knowledge of how to swim nor a saddle for me to sit on. When I look back now I'm certain my guardian angel never had a minute of rest.

My sadness over the lost horse was quickly replaced by the potential fun that I could have with the German kids in the neighborhood, especially since they didn't speak Romany, and I spoke both their and my language.

What I had not figured was that with the additional living space, now that we were in a flat instead of the wagon, additional chores around the house would arise. Before, Mother had insisted that we all leave the wagon when she cleaned, with the exception of my two oldest sisters, who would do the dishes. Now she insisted that the cleaning up of the flat was the responsibility of everyone. Of course, father was exempt from his responsibility.

Sometimes, though, I was allowed to go with my grandparents who still traveled on business all over Germany. Grandpa would check to see that the baskets and chairs which they had made over the long winter months were secured tightly. Then we would climb into the wagon and be off to sell their wares.

However, settling down did not guarantee that the Gypsy would be free from harassment. Sometimes Gypsies were accused of being spies or disloyal to the state—especially in the Germanic states. As early as 1899, a Gypsy Information Service (*Zigeunernachrichtsdienst*) had been established in Munich, Bavaria, and in 1905, the Bavarian government had published a "Gypsy Book" of acts and edicts from 1816 to 1903 which related to Gypsies. This had been compiled to serve as guidelines against the Gypsy Plague (*Zigeunerplage*) and would be used for continued persecution in the twentieth century. Information was collected and stored on Gypsy individuals and families, and fingerprinting of all Gypsies, particularly those who were settled and came in contact regularly with the German authorities, was introduced shortly after World War I.[35]

France had enacted legislation requiring all Gypsies who lacked French citizenship to carry identification papers which required such specific details as the size of head, length of right ear, length of left foot. (Germany required a similar identification in 1922.) Shortly thereafter regulations appeared in most European countries forbidding Gypsies to travel and camp in family groups. They could not own sporting guns or other firearms in Bavaria. In addition, Gypsies over sixteen years of age without regular employment could be sent to workhouses.[36]

Perhaps one of the greatest ironies was that the Gypsies, always accused of stealing the Gaje's children, had their own children removed from them by the authorities in several countries. In Hungary government officials took Gypsy children from their parents so that the children could be reared by Christian people. German authorities attempted to take by force all children of Gypsy families in the area of Norhausen and place them in an institution. The Norwegians tried similar action, declaring that it was unhealthy for the Gypsy children to live in tents and wagons, and, in 1930, a Norwegian writer demanded that Gypsies throughout Norway be sterilized.[37] However, these centuries of anti-Gypsy sentiment, discrimination, and persecution would escalate and soon be surpassed during the era of Germany's Third Reich.

Two

∾

Ominous Signs

On Wednesday... the first concentration camp will be opened in the vicinity of Dachau.... We have adopted this measure, undeterred by paltry scruples, in the conviction that our action will help to restore calm to our country and is in the best interest of our people.

—*Die Münchner Neuesten Nachrichten*
(*Munich's Latest News*), March 1933

Who could anticipate the anguish this obscure announcement would bring to so many Europeans in just a few short years? Even the best educated and politically astute could not, or would not, comprehend the full meaning of this message from the new Nazi regime. Certainly, those most likely to be unaware were the Gypsies—misfits in European society, detached from Gaje government, powerless, and generally illiterate.

Pollo R. was one of the few Gypsy youngsters regularly enrolled in school, and it was there that he would first feel the tides of unrest about to engulf him, his family, Europe, and the world. "I had thoroughly enjoyed my first three years of school," Pollo recalled. However, when he began fourth grade shortly after Easter in 1939, his joy turned into despair and anger.

> Mr. Baruk, the principal of the school, had become not only my teacher but also my daily tormentor. My mental anguish began when he had banished me from the front of the classroom to the back row. While I had been encouraged prior to fourth grade to participate, Mr. Baruk not only discouraged me, but forbade me to either ask or answer questions.

After an initial period of showing his dislike for Pollo by totally ignoring his presence, Baruk began to verbalize his aversion. The boy decided against mentioning the problem to his mother as she was very worried about his father who was an artilleryman in the Wehrmacht, fighting in Poland.

Then one day, in front of the entire class, he said to me, "You filthy Gypsy! You must go to Poland and trade with horse tails! You don't belong here. You belong with filth. Turn your face to the corner; we don't want to see your ugly Gypsy face."

My anger against him had reached its apex, and I screamed, "You are the Polack, not me! I was born here. Why don't you go to Poland?" Mr. Baruk practically raced to the front of the classroom, got a heavy stick and began beating me about my shoulders.

Pollo ran from the classroom. When he arrived home, he discovered that his older brother, Thomas, was home on furlough from the Polish campaign. Sobbing, he explained Mr. Baruk's insults and how the incident had escalated.

Thomas listened very attentively. Then he dressed in his full military uniform. I shall never forget it. He buckled on his holster with its 3.08 pistol. Never speaking a word, he grabbed my hand, and we walked to the school. Mr. Baruk was standing by the blackboard. Thomas hit him so hard that he fell against the blackboard and it broke. Then Thomas shouted, "You damn Polack! We have to get coals out of the fire [fight your war] for you dirt bags and on top of that we are insulted and our children are beaten. Well, not with this family you damn Nazi Schwein!"

The incident was immediately reported to the authorities. Later that evening Thomas was arrested by the Gestapo and sent to a penal battalion in Sulvalki, Poland. He was never heard from again. Mr. Baruk was hospitalized for several months because of the beating by Thomas, another instructor was hired to take his place, and Pollo returned to the classroom. Still, Pollo's formal education would end before the year was over. It was shortly before Christmas, when one day the substitute for Mr. Baruk announced:

"Pollo, take your rucksack and leave the school grounds."

"But I did not do anything," I replied, tears running down my face.

"You are a Gypsy, are you not?" the teacher asked.

"Yes, but..." I was not even allowed to finish my sentence when the teacher began yelling, "Then out of here; we have no space for your kind."

Pollo R.'s experience would become typical as German schools prohibited Jews and Gypsies from attendance.

Like other targeted groups deemed a threat to the Third Reich, the Gypsies were on the brink of the holocaust—that senseless and inhumane persecution which was beginning to surface throughout Nazi Germany and all of Europe. Although the Gypsies have been among the least visible victims of the holocaust and little historical material is available to document the cases of Rom persecution and death, some sources feel their decimation was far greater than that of the Jews or other "unacceptable" minorities.

Most historians writing about the holocaust indicate that the Nazi campaign against the Gypsies differed from that of other sufferers and that the fate of the Jews was unique. These scholars imply that the Gypsy involvement in the holocaust was merely accidental—an afterthought. This idea is difficult to support, however, as the Gypsy persecution in the Germany of the 1930s and 1940s was inexorably tied to all those individuals who were said to be a threat to the Aryan community because of criminality, mental illness, physical handicaps, "racial impurities," and "alien blood." Included in this "racial" category along with the Gypsies were Jews and those with Negro heritage—mainly mulatto children who had been born of German women and African French colonial soldiers on occupation duty in Germany after the First World War.

Several scholars of the holocaust have also indicated that the restrictive laws involving the Gypsies were in no way connected to the issue of race. Again, their stand is difficult to support. Eugenics and racial laws passed or measures taken against the Jews were nearly simultaneously incorporated against the Gypsies and other "asocials." The Third Reich was fascinated with the idea of preserving the purity of German blood. In 1938, a year before the outbreak of World War II, Adolph Wirth, a member of a racial research team headed by neurologist and pediatrician Dr. Robert Ritter, wrote:

The Gypsy Question is today in the first place a racial question. Just as the National Socialist State has solved the Jewish Question, so it will have to fundamentally regulate the Gypsy Question.... In the regulation for the implementation of the Nuremberg Laws for the protection of German blood, Gypsies have been placed on an equal level with the Jews in regard to marriage prohibitions.... [T]hey count neither as of German blood or related to it.[1]

This attitude may have been tied in to earlier ideas that Gypsies and Jews were actually one people. Investigations and writings from the seventeenth century had linked Gypsies to the Jews. A thesis by German writer Johann Christof Wagenseil (printed in 1697) attempted to prove that "the very first Gypsies were Jews who stemmed from Germany." Other statements from German scholars such as, "In Europe generally only Jews and Gypsies are of foreign blood," and, "Apart from the Jews, only the Gypsies come into consideration in Europe as members of an alien people,"[2] made the destinies of the two minorities inseparable. Because some Germans in the 1930s thought there might be some racial affinity to Jews, the Reichszentrale zur Bekämpfung des Zigeunerwesens and Rassen-hygienische Forschungsstelle agencies began research on this subject.[3]

THE QUESTION OF RACIAL PURITY

At various times, and depending upon who was involved, the Nazi attitude toward the Gypsies was somewhat ambivalent. Racial purity, an important part of Nazi philosophy, placed the "Aryan" Germans at the top of the racial hierarchy; yet there was some discussion that the Gypsies were racially pure, possibly of Aryan descent. Romany had been designated an Aryan language, and some scholars felt that "pure" Gypsies might have a Nordic heritage. If these suppositions were fact, then the Gypsies would be an "acceptable" people.

However, these suppositions were short-lived, and Nazi scientists were soon to conclude otherwise. While anthropologist Professor Hans F. K. Guenther commented that the Gypsies might have retained some elements from their Nordic home, he went on to emphasize "they are descended from the lowest classes of the population in that region." Another scientist indicated that the Gypsies' Asiatic ancestors "were totally different from our Nordic forefathers."[4] Guenther also concluded that as a result of their nomadic lifestyle, the Gypsies had become a mixture of Oriental, Western, Asiatic, Indian, mid-Asiatic, and European strains and wrote, "The Gypsies will generally affect Europe as aliens."[5] Because of these and similar arguments, the Gypsy population in Germany was finally branded by the Nazis as non-Aryan.

Although the Nazis were probably not overly concerned about justifying a "Gypsy menace" solely on the basis that the Gypsies had been classified non-Aryan, their arguments against the Gypsies also involved the obsessive German concern with "health" and "purity." A 1938 document from Portschy, the Nazi Gauleiter of Steiermark, to Reichminister Dr. Heinz Lammers indicated that Gypsies had a "foul heredity and were described as habitual criminals and parasites imperiling German racial purity."[6]

Laws had already been passed in Germany in the early 1930s which made non-Europeans second-class citizens.[7] The Law to Prevent Offspring with Hereditary Defects (July 1933), the Regulation for the Security and Reform of Habitual Criminals and Social Deviants (November 1933), and the Law for Marriage Health (October 1935) were passed to exclude mental patients, the institutionalized handicapped, and social deviants from the Nazis' biologically homogeneous society. Both Gypsies and Jews fell into at least one of these categories.

In 1935, the Nuremberg Law for the Protection of Blood and Honor made unions between Gypsies and non-Gypsies illegal on racial grounds. The miscegenation clauses of the Nuremberg Laws were applied to both Romany and Sinti Gypsies; in addition, clauses in the other laws against habitual criminals, social misfits, vagabonds and asocials were brought to bear in the campaign to rid Germany of the Gypsy menace.[8] It must be emphasized again, however, that the Nazi concept of criminality or the label "asocial" became a racial category as it applied to Gypsies. Heinrich Himmler emphasized in 1938 that based on eugenic research, any solution to the Gypsy Plague "must be approached with the basic nature of this race in mind."[9]

Certainly the Nazis had been proposing various solutions to the Gypsy menace for quite some time. Shortly after Hitler came to power in 1933, "a special SS study group was tasked to make suggestions on how to solve the Gypsy problem."[10] One of the suggestions for solving the problem involved mass sterilization of the Gypsies.

STERILIZATION

Sterilization was continually mentioned by scientists and public officials in Germany as a way to prevent additional Gypsy offspring. In the first year of Nazi rule, a law calling for the prevention of hereditarily diseased offspring had been enacted. This, coupled with edicts later in the year, allowed some non-Gypsy travelers and some asocial persons to be sterilized.

Although records are sparse, indications are that as early as 1933 (the same year Munich's newspaper indicated a concentration camp would be opened near Dachau), the German police confined many Gypsies in special camps called *Zigeunerlager*. The Office for Research on Race, Hygiene, and Population Biology in the Reich Department of Health began the racial and genealogical registration of all Gypsies in the Zigeunerlager. Frequently, this registration resulted in loss of citizenship and involuntary sterilization.[11]Another early law (1933) which permitted sterilization of the mentally deficient later came to encompass Gypsies of mixed blood.[12]

And this concept of mixed blood apparently was not the same for all groups. The definition of a "Gypsy mixture" was much narrower than that of a "half-Jew." One was considered to be Gypsy mixture if one had at least two Gypsy-mixtures as ancestors. In other words, when two of a person's sixteen great-grandparents were Roma, that person was classified as "Gypsy-mixture." (From 1943 on, because of that classification, those individuals could be deported to Auschwitz.)[13]

At first, there appears to have been more leniency given in regard to Jewish blood than to Gypsy blood when individuals were selected to be incarcerated. A person with a Jewish grandparent (one out of four great-grandparents) initially was not touched by the anti-Jewish laws. For example, an individual with less than one-quarter Jewish heritage was less likely to be deported to a concentration camp.[14] On the other hand, an individual with as little as an eighth Gypsy heritage was almost certain to be deported or interned.

If a Gypsy became involved with the police, enforced sterilization was always a possibility. In 1935, Bader, a high-ranking member of the German police, suggested that for any Gypsy who disturbed public order or broke the law, no mercy be considered and, "It might be worth considering including such Gypsies under those persons affected by the Sterilization Law."[15] A 1937 German announcement was also made that "99% of the Roma children are ready to be sterilized."[16]

Between 1937 and 1944 Dr. Ritter (who would eventually head the Office for Race, Hygiene, and Population Biology) received considerable funding from the German government for various genealogic and anthropologic investigations on Gypsies and Jews, including his "Studies on asocial individuals and on the biology of bastards." This work supposedly "confirmed" Ritter's 1935 hypothesis that most of the 30,000 Gypsies in Germany according to classifications he had established were not really Gypsies at all but "the products of matings with the German criminal asocial subproletariat."[17] Ritter proposed that Gypsies be prevented from mixing with people of "German blood," that "pure" Gypsies be separated from Gypsies of mixed blood (*Mischlinge*), that sterilization be performed on the Mischlinge, and that they be put in forced labor camps.[18]

Another scientist, Eva Justin, also made a study for future racial hygienic laws which she hoped would prevent a further flow of "unworthy primitive elements" into the German population. After studying 148 Gypsy children of mixed blood, she concluded that their morals were unacceptable, that they could not be integrated into German society because of their primitive ways of thinking, and that "[a]ll educated Gypsies and part-Gypsies of predominantly Gypsy blood, whether socially assimilated or asocial and criminal, should as a general rule be sterilized."[19]

A state secretary of the Reich Ministry of the Interior wrote to the Head Office of the Security of Police in 1940 stating that he was "convinced that a definitive solution to the Gypsy problem can only be achieved by making Gypsies and part-Gypsies infertile."[20] When, in 1940, Gypsies were collected for relocation to Polish occupied areas, adults had to sign a statement indicating, "I was told today that in the case of my forbidden return to Germany, I will be sterilized and be in preventive incarceration (concentration camp).[21] Certainly anyone who has read the above comments must see that for the Nazis the Gypsy problem was also considered to be a racial problem.

OTHER REPRESSIVE MEASURES

While the proposed mass sterilization of Gypsies would be delayed, under Heinrich Himmler (Reichsführer-SS, who was the head of the entire German police system) and Reinhard Heydrich (the head of criminal investigation and the Gestapo) many restrictive edicts against the Gypsies would soon take effect.

As early as November 18, 1936, an order entitled *Bekämpfung des Zigeunerunwesens* (Fight Against the Gypsy Existence) directed German police to collect the following information on all Gypsies in their areas:

1. Where the Gypsies were residing.
2. Names of families and the number of family members.
3. When the Gypsy families had arrived in the specific locations.[22]

On December 14, 1937, a law was passed whereby Gypsies who were without an occupation, were habitual criminals, or were a threat to society through their asocial behavior could be taken into protective custody, whether they had committed any crime or not.[23]

On December 8, 1938, a decree upholding "the fight against the Gypsy plague" clearly spoke on the *solution* to the issue of the Gypsy question. All Gypsies above the age of six were ordered to submit themselves to race biological judgment by the official Gypsy research institute. Although most readers might assume that Gypsies were interned only after World War II began, Gypsies and Gypsy-hybrids (some who were accused of having intercourse with "Germanblooded") were incarcerated in concentration camps in September, 1939, long before the "official" beginning of World War II. The director of the Dachau museum has determined that the first Gypsy prisoners were brought to Dachau concentration camp near Munich in 1938.[24] However, one source puts the date of internment much earlier, indicating that by the end of 1936, great numbers of Gypsies went to Dachau, Sachsenhausen, and Buchenwald "under the cloak of the fight against asocials and criminals."[25]

Lena Winterstein remembered that her husband was among those sent to Dachau in 1938 (and then on to Mauthausen).[26] A German civilian also recalled some of the Gypsy names in Dachau: Horvath, Scharkosi, Baranai. They were "jolly fellows...mostly from Austria, about 2,000."[27] The actions of the Germans at this time were certainly incongruous, for while all of these repressive measures were being carried out against Romany families, the German government continued conscription of many Gypsy men into the Wehrmacht.

The ban on Gypsy children attending school began in 1939. For example, from February 1939 on, only one school grade existed in all of the city of Cologne for all Roma children. A "teacher shortage" was the reason given to exclude Gypsy children from Frankfurt schools in early 1941. In March 1941, the secretary for education decreed that Roma who were without German citizenship would no longer be allowed to attend German schools.[28]

Deportation was another tool used by the Nazis to control or eliminate the Gypsy population. On September 21, 1939, Heydrich had organized a meeting at which the participants decided that 30,000 Gypsies, from Greater Germany, West Prussia, and the Warthe region, should be deported from Germany and those sections of Poland under control of the Reich. Deportees would be removed to a part of Poland (not incorporated into the Reich) which was designated as the General Government. Apparently, transportation was unavailable at that time, however, and deportation of most Gypsies was delayed until the spring of 1940.[29]

Following Heydrich's meeting, on October 17, 1939, a census was ordered to be conducted from October 25 to 27 of all Gypsies and Gypsy hybrids. (Pollo R.'s family was registered during this census.) In addition, the October 17 Settlement Order issued by Heydrich prohibited Gypsies from leaving their current habitats, and local police were instructed to set up concentration camps for later apprehension of this segment of the population. Following the census, on November 20, 1939, all Gypsy women who were involved in the practice of clairvoyance or fortune-telling were to be deported immediately to concentration camps.[30]

For those Gypsies who would escape the original roundup and remain relatively free over a period of time, and even for those who were interned and awaiting resettlement, the harassment continued. Although the Gypsies needed to engage in some form of work in order to keep an income, special work cards were issued in late 1939, severely limiting their employment; all other previously issued cards or permits were confiscated, leaving them without proof of citizenship. In early 1942, like the Jews, those

Gypsies fortunate enough not to be interned and to be still employed lost rights to sick leave and holidays. Also, they were taxed on their income an additional 15 percent above regular taxes and deductions.[31]

Was there resistance to the growing persecution of the Gypsies? Kenrick and Puxon mention Dr. Sigmund Wolf, a Gypsy scholar, who apparently offered some opposition. When the Nazis came to power Wolf was regularly sent lists of Gypsy names by the Party Information Service and the Central Office in Munich and asked to trace the genealogy of these families. Eventually, Wolf was approached by Dr. Achim Gerche, a genealogy expert working in the Ministry of the Interior. Gerche asked Wolf to send him any Gypsy genealogy lists he had made and also to come to work for him at the Ministry. Dr. Wolf refused both requests, a refusal which did not go unpunished. In 1936, the doctor's "home in Magdeburg was raided and all his material was taken away by the Gestapo.... He was later informed that his material was being used by a Dr. Ritter and that he would be put in a concentration camp if he continued to protest about the affair."[32] Surely there must have been other men in Germany of good conscience who made protests, but if there were, they either were themselves interned or records of their protests were destroyed.

However, as later became evident, the arrests, confinement, and general discrimination were only a prelude to further Gypsy persecution. And it was not only in Germany that Gypsies were being rounded up, deported, or interned. In Poland, Yugoslavia, Hungary, France, and the rest of continental Europe, civilian as well as military authorities used the war as an excuse to eliminate their "Gypsy problems." In Serbia, the German military commander ordered in May 1941, that all property of Jews and Gypsies be confiscated. In Poland, Gypsies were being confined to Jewish ghettos.[33] Harassment was everywhere.

No Place of Refuge

Again and again, the question is raised: What caused these groups either to fail or refuse to recognize the ominous signs which led to victimization, arrest, internment, and, eventually, annihilation? The answer for the Gypsies is complex and involves many elements of both German society and the Gypsy subculture.

In 1933, when the Nazi party came to power in Germany, it had (as is shown in chapter one) extensive precedence in European law for subverting the Gypsy population. The Nazis had but to adapt these laws to their purposes.

Making the Nazis' job easier during this time was the distrust and dislike between the various groups targeted for persecution. Had they recognized the persecution as a common threat, the entire holocaust outcome might have been different. In general, the German populace (including many of the Jews, blacks, and other ethnic groups which would also suffer at the hands of the Nazis) were hostile to or, at best, ambivalent toward the plight of the Gypsies and took little interest in laws affecting what they considered to be an undesirable element. Most felt that harassing or banning a Gypsy child like Pollo R. from school was of little consequence as it tended to keep the riffraff away from the upstanding German citizens.

It is not so hard, then, to understand how European Gypsies became victims of the holocaust. There had always been a "Gypsy menace" as far as most Europeans were concerned; the Gypsies were aware of and had lived with persecution and discrimination for hundreds of years, so they expected discriminatory conduct from the Gaje. While they were somewhat economically dependent upon the dominant Gaje culture, they were accustomed to being second-class people, existing with a relative degree of comfort within the closeness of their isolated Gypsy subculture and detached from the political ploys of German society. Like others who had been classified "asocial" by the Nazis and took no responsive action, it would have been virtually impossible for Gypsies to imagine that, while they went about their daily routines in the cities or roamed the byways of Poland, Germany, France, or Yugoslavia, concentration camps were being erected to detain them and mass extermination was in their future.

Although some Gypsies (mainly the Sinti in Germany and the Lallari in Austria) had settled into a more sedentary lifestyle, many of the Rom continued their nomadic ways. Therefore, unlike Pollo R., few were in an area long enough to receive much schooling nor was education considered of prime importance. Most could not have read the decrees issued against them, even if they had been aware of their publication. This lack of literacy coupled with their general suspicion of the Gaje society effectively separated them from the normal channels of communication. Even if some concerned Gaje had thought to warn them of impending doom, most would have been suspicious and would not have accepted this information as trustworthy.

It is easy to use hindsight and ask, "Why didn't the Gypsies leave Europe when resettlement began?" However, this question merely raises more questions. Where would they have gone? What country would have taken them in? What economic resources were available to them?

In addition, like the Jews, the Gypsies' response usually is that their roots and their "home" were in Europe. Whether they were living in towns or meandering from one Gypsy encampment to another, their friends and relatives were, and had been, a part of the European scene for ten centuries. As Katja H., a German Sinti now living in America said, "Like the Jews, we had homes there, businesses. We Sinti were upstanding Germans; we didn't think anything could happen to us. We were reared in Germany; it was our home. We thought of ourselves as Germans."

Abandoning this heritage and attempting to migrate to another country was probably never given any serious consideration. Behind them lay their centuries-long history of persecution by dominant European groups. So far they had survived that history. They either could not comprehend their impending doom or could not see a way to escape it.

Three

❧

A Deadly Journey

The resettlement decree from 27 April 1940 ordered that 2,500 Gypsies were to be deported [to Poland]...
—Tilman Zülch, *In Auschwitz Vergast bis Heute Verfolgt*

From various parts of the Reich these first Gypsies were collected—snatched from their homes in the middle of the night. Dazed and disoriented, they offered no resistance as they were transported across the European countryside. One thousand from Hamburg and Bremen; 1,000 from Cologne, Düsseldorf, and Hanover; 500 from Stuttgart and Frankfurt. They were numbered, deloused, and then loaded onto cattle cars—50 to a car. Records indicate that the 1,000 from Hamburg helped construct a "forest camp" in Poland and then were released for a short period of time. The 500 from Stuttgart were reported to have gone to the Judenstadt (Jewish city) of Czenzidjow. Little is known of the 1,000 Gypsies who were transported from Cologne.[1] However, Pollo R. was among those on the Cologne transport and recalled the days leading up to his family's resettlement:

> Unacquainted to reading and writing, we were unable to pick up a newspaper to read what was going on in our country. No one said anything to us as far as I knew. However, after the census in October 1939, Mother knew instinctively that all was not well for us. While she had earned a few pennies reading other people's fortunes, she had been ordered by the Gestapo to stop this under the threat of being deported to a concentration camp. Furthermore effective immediately, we were no longer allowed to leave our home. By now, even we children knew that something was terribly wrong, for we were no longer allowed to attend school.

Pollo's father, Hans R., and five older brothers, who had been conscripted in 1938, were still serving in the German Army. At the beginning of
May 1940, Hans returned from the campaign in Poland. All of the family
were very proud of him as he had received a high war decoration, the Iron
Cross first class. They were still getting accustomed to the idea of having
him home when at 4:00 A.M. on May 15, 1940, someone knocked loudly on
the door.

> The Gestapo dropped in for a visit. They awakened me and my
> brothers by kicking in the bedroom door. They told us to get into the
> living room and be ready to travel in five minutes.
>
> With the Gestapo was a detective who had been an acquaintance
> of Father's. He explained to Father that the family was going to be
> evacuated to the other side of the Rhine river for safety reasons,
> because Krefeld (the family's home town) might be a target for bomb-
> ing. We were only to take twenty pounds of clothes and would be given
> blankets and the like upon our arrival.
>
> The detective's explanation sounded reasonable to my father,
> and none of the other men seemed receptive to questions. With prod-
> ding from Father we scurried to dress and sort out what we could take
> from what must be abandoned. We thought that surely the evacuation
> period would not be long. Father and Mother tried to calm us children.

Each member of Pollo's family was handed an identification card
which had a large "R U" stamped across it. (Later family members would
learn that R U stood for Rückkehr Unerwünscht—Return Undesired). The
family was loaded into the back of a covered truck which immediately left
Krefeld. On their journey, the truck stopped once to pick up another Gypsy
family and then continued on to Cologne. Pollo, who was just twelve years
old at the time, recalled that he and the younger children were extremely
frightened.

> Never before in my life had I seen so many people all in one
> place. All of the people appeared to be Gypsies, just like us. Upon our
> arrival, the Nazis took photographs of our entire family, fingerprinted
> each of us, and checked our mouths for gold teeth.
>
> Since Mother was only half Gypsy, the Nazis offered her free-
> dom if she would divorce our father. She declined. But even when we
> arrived in Cologne to be interned with thousands of other Gypsies and

had all of this done to us, I think we did not comprehend the horrors that lay ahead of us.

Thus Selma R. (Pollo's mother), who was only part Gypsy was given a chance at freedom, but she refused the offer. She would stay with her family.

Also, Gypsies married to a German citizen or Gypsy families with a father or son in the German armed forces were supposedly excluded from deportation.[2] Hans R. carefully explained his family's participation in Germany's recent conquest of Poland.

> I have served my country well; I have here my Iron Cross for dedication and valor. My sons here were also in the Wehrmacht. One of my sons is still in the East [Poland]. Does not that prove we have faithfully served Germany?

Hans' military service was ignored. While for some Gypsies, on a sort of hit-or-miss basis, the rule of exclusion was applied, his entire family was scheduled for relocation.

Hitler's "ethnic cleansing" and resettlement of the Gypsies, which began with a speed characteristic of his Blitzkrieg, would be continuous throughout Europe from May 1940 until the end of World War II. This group, categorized as a "parasitical people leading a parasitical life" included persons who looked like Gypsies or wandered around in a "Gypsy-like" manner. Once rounded up they were then put into several classifications:

Z   Full Gypsy (*Zigeuner*)
ZM+   Gypsy *Mischling*, predominantly Gypsy
ZM   Gypsy *Mischling* with equal Gypsy and German "blood shares"
ZM-   Gypsy *Mischling*, predominantly German
NZ   Free of Gypsy Blood[3]

Although the initial roundup of Gypsies sent to Cologne appears to be well organized and well documented, apparently this was the exception rather than the rule. Instead of orders coming directly from those at the top of the government, many times a city or county government would decide on the date and method to be used in gathering together various clans of Gypsies. Again, the times for collection and those individuals to be included varied. Sinti and Lalleri were often excluded, at least in the early roundups. In addition, although the Gypsies in that first group taken to Cologne were for the most part "settled" families with permanent addresses in the city, not all of the Rom were as accessible; many were still nomadic, changing their habitat daily or weekly and making collection for resettlement very difficult. Because of their continuing mobility, many had not been counted in the 1938 census, and records on their whereabouts, their exact numbers in the various European nations, or the numbers of those captured are unreliable.

Unlike the Jews, many of whom were highly educated and managed to leave behind diaries and lists of those imprisoned and killed, an accurate accounting for the Gypsies is extremely difficult. In addition, once internment, resettlement, and execution of Gypsies began in Germany and Poland, many other countries initiated similar measures against their Gypsy population. These countries also did not keep detailed accounts of those Gypsies who died in camp, were murdered by the native population, or were deported to camps in Germany and Poland.

Then, too, it must be remembered that Nazi Germany did not conquer and occupy all European countries at the same time. For example, while Poland was invaded in September 1939, Yugoslavia was not attacked until October 1940, nor Greece until April 1941. (See appendix.) Because of this fact, there are fascinating and almost unexplainable stories of a few Gypsies who eluded capture for several years by moving from country to country, who were rounded up and then set free, or who managed to escape from concentration camps, at least for a period of time.

Instructions for the roundup of "undesirables" were explicitly stated: Polish Jews were to be moved into cities. Jews in the Reich were to be moved to Poland. The 30,000 Gypsies in the Reich also were to be moved to Poland. Why the figure of 30,000 Gypsies was used is unclear. Supposedly the number of registered Gypsies still in Germany in late 1939 was somewhere between 34,000 and 40,000. Two German statisticians, Dr. Wetzel and Dr. Hecht, who were working on projecting the numbers of future victims, indicated in a November 5, 1939, document that 100,000 Gypsies and others were scheduled for deportation to Poland at that time. Possibly the numbers vary because of those sent to Dachau in 1936 and 1938 or, although unsupported by written evidence, because of reports from various sources of "trains packed with Gypsies, rolling towards Poland, from the autumn of 1939."[4]

An SS Standartenführer, Otto Ohlendorff, claimed at the Nuremberg trials that he had on his conscience the murder of 90,000 Jews and Gypsies. How many of this number were Gypsies is not clearly stated. During three days in November 1941, records indicate that five thousand Gypsies were deported to Lodz in Poland; however, it is not definitely known if this number is representative of additional days or of deportations to other camps. Although no numbers were given, SS Standartenführer Darmzog also stated that in a province which he headed "the Gypsy population was especially quickly dealt with."[5] It is not documented whether this referred to annihilation or deportation. But while the total number of Gypsies rounded up and interned has not been determined, most sources indicate there were hundreds of thousands, and the horror of those days is relived by the survivors.

THE TREKS BEGIN

Some sources divide the organized arrests, confinements, and exterminations into three major waves—the first in Germany and Austria, the second in the invaded lands of Poland, the Soviet Union, Holland, France, etc., and the third, in Hungary, Rumania, and Bulgaria. Lena Winterstein[6] recalled that her family (except for her husband, who had been sent to Dachau in 1938) were rounded up in the first wave in 1940.

> I think we all got sent to Hohenastberg [near Stuttgart] where we all were numbered. Then we were sent off approximately eight to fourteen days later to Poland. There we were distributed to different camps.

The family of Pollo R. also was caught up in the first wave and began a series of numerous moves from camp to camp, a predicament which faced many of the Gypsy internees all through the war years. From their initial internment point in Cologne, family members were transported first to the small village of Platerowa on the border between Poland and Russia, where they lived for approximately nine months. Their stay was not to be a permanent one. Shortly after the beginning of 1941, all of the Gypsies at Platerowa were told they must move. No vehicles were available for transportation, so the group had to walk a combined distance of over 400 miles, from Platerowa to Krakow and, finally, to the Warsaw ghetto. Pollo recalled what seemed like an endless trek.

> It was so very cold. There was snow and we didn't have shoes. The lucky ones had sacks tied around their feet. The others had bare feet. We slept under the heavens. We were always hungry.
>
> When we started there were fourteen of us. But on the way my smaller brother Robert, who was about eight or nine, got frostbitten feet. He became very ill and we could do nothing for him. We had no medical supplies on hand; no doctor was there to help him. Finally, he died. But we had nowhere to bury him except just beside the road in a shallow grave. My mother was determined not to leave him behind. She kept saying that the wolves might get his body.
>
> So even though we were all very weak and suffering from the cold, we took turns carrying him. His arms and legs were running with pus; they were gangrenous, and the odor from them was something terrible. Still, my mother insisted that we not put him down beside the road. Finally, when we got to our destination at the ghetto, he was put in a coffin-like box. But we never actually saw that he got buried.

Wanda G.,[7] a German Sinti, also recalled the events leading up to her roundup and arrival at Auschwitz-Birkenau:

> It must have been early Spring 1942. I was either twelve or thirteen years old. I knew my birthday was April 15, but I had lost track of time. After we all had been apprehended by the Gestapo, we smaller children got separated from our parents. At first we were placed in an orphanage.

As "undesirables," the Gypsy children were not allowed to stay with the other children in the orphanage but were housed in a cellar. Late each evening, when it was already dark, a woman whom Wanda described as a nurse would come and lead the Gypsies outside to get fresh air and some exercise.

> One day, we were told to take everything with us for we would not return to the cellar. The joy was great when a woman dressed in a Red Cross outfit told us that we would go on a train ride. Despite our nagging questions, where we were going to, would we see our parents,

we were not told anything. But what difference would it have made if they had told us, for we children did not know what the Gypsy camp in Auschwitz-Birkenau was, but we would soon learn all about it.

As quickly as possible, the Germans got rid of their Gypsy problem. However, it was not only in Germany where the roundups and internment occurred. Nowhere in Europe would Gypsies really be safe.

CONQUERED TERRITORIES

Still reeling from the speed of the German invasion, the bewildered populations of the subdued nations generally were too caught up in their own troubles to take notice of what was happening to Gypsies in their country. Nevertheless, for those interested in ridding their country of any "asocials," the turmoil of the times provided an excuse for swiftly collecting and confining these unwanted people.

The Gypsy policy in occupied territories was similar to that in Germany—to intern the Gypsies in holding camps and then transport them to Germany, where, most often, they were moved on to Poland for forced labor or extermination. Outside of Germany, this second wave of arrests, confinement, and persecution began around 1941 in the invaded lands of Belgium, Holland, Poland, the Soviet Union, Italy, and France.

Perhaps it was not too difficult for France to follow Germany's leadership regarding internment of Gypsies. Even *before* the German occupation of France in 1940, the French government considered the Gypsies a plague on their society, denied them the right to travel, and placed them under police surveillance. If police caught the Rom on the road, it was easy to order them into designated camps. Once in these camps, they were placed in compulsory employment.[8]

Between July and October 1940, Alsace-Lorraine solved its problem with Jews, asocials, and Gypsies by moving them out of their territory and dumping them on country roads in other parts of France.[9] In both Alsace and Lorraine, Gypsy groups were to be disbanded, fortune-tellers arrested, and those unemployed treated as asocials. Some Gypsies became victims of battles, killed by French soldiers when caught between retreating French and advancing German units. When France was finally divided between the German Administration in the north and the Vichy Zone in the south, internment camps multiplied and soon held 30,000 Gypsy internees. It is interesting to note that the supervision of these Gypsy camps rested with a part of the bureaucracy known as the French Ministry for Jewish Questions.[10] Apparently, the two ethnic minorities were simply lumped together.

While Pollo's family in Germany had been allowed to take a few of their personal effects, this was not always the case in France. One group of 212 Gypsies arrived at the French compound of Montreuil in December 1941, without any luggage or winter clothes. A medical report from the camp further indicated "[T]here is little wood available for heating."[11]

Apparently, the French government is still reticent today about French involvement in these camps and the conditions under which the Gypsies lived. There were, however, some twenty large camps and many smaller ones, including three special camps for Gypsy children. In addition to Montreuil, others included those at Angoulême, Renner, Poitiers, Compiegne, Moison-la-Rivière, Noe, Coudrescieux, and numerous other locations throughout Alsace-Lorraine and central and Vichy France.[12]

Thousands of Gypsies were simply stopped on the highways and immediately interned. A French Gypsy named German Campos recalled that she and her family were arrested in March 1941. Even though her father was a naturalized French citizen and had reared thirteen children in France, the family was taken to a camp at Rivensalter. Like many of the Gypsy families, they would then be moved to a second camp and then a third. Finally they were released in September 1944.[13]

Some French Gypsies were not as "lucky" as the Campos. At age twelve Paul Wanderstein survived the massacre of his family near the village of Saint Sixte. German soldiers took fourteen of the Gypsies from their camp to a field to be shot—Paul's mother, two sisters, his grandmother, an uncle, and cousins.

> Two of them and one of my girl cousins lay only wounded but appeared dead. Three others escaped by running into the village and hiding in the school loft. I don't remember exactly what happened but I was concealed somehow in the village and saved.[14]

Just to the south of France, the Gypsies were also at risk. In Italy, under Mussolini, large-scale roundups of Gypsies were being carried out.

Some of these roundups also occurred before World War II began. Families were first collected in staging camps and then transported to islands surrounding Italy. Like the Germans, the Italians needed men for their military. At the same time that their families were being interned, Gyspy males were being conscripted into the Italian army. Some of these troops participated in the Italian invasion of Albania and were ordered not to return to Italy. Since many of the wives and children followed the men to Albania, the Italian Fascists were able to rid the country of quite a few unwanted Gypsy families.[15]

Gypsies were to face similar fates in the Low Countries. Those registered by the Dutch police were picked up in a special sweep, interned at Westerbork, Holland, and transferred to Auschwitz. There were at least a few Gypsy prisoners from Luxembourg, for Adolf Eichmann mentioned them during his trial in Israel. Although records indicate the number from Belgium was also small, some Gypsies were arrested and held for transport to the East. Marie Maitre, a Belgian survivor, was moved first to Malines, then to Auschwitz, Ravensbrück, and Buchenwald. "Only eight other Gypsies of those sent to Auschwitz from Belgium lived."[16]

While a great number of Polish Gypsies were interned in the Warsaw ghetto or Auschwitz, thousands did not survive the initial roundup. Many were shot upon capture by local police or gendarmes. In the Krakow district, close to 1,000 were shot, about 100 were shot in the county of Radomsk as late as 1943, and reports indicate that hundreds of Gypsy families were also shot in the Warsaw district.[17]

The Gypsies were not spared in the genocide that overtook large segments of the Russian population. In the invaded areas of the Soviet Union, German special operation units known as the Einsatzgruppen were told to exterminate Gypsies at the same time and in the same way as they exterminated the Jews. Artur Nebe, commander of Einsatzgruppe B, operating out of White Russia (Byelorussia), wrote to the SS Medical Service and offered to send "asocial Gypsy half-breeds" for experiments in drinking seawater.[18] A report dispatched by the Geheime Feldpolizei (secret army field police), in August 1942, stated that roaming bands of Gypsies should be "ruthlessly exterminated." It is also believed that, along with Jews, Gypsies were victims at Babi Yar near Kiev.[19] Located in the Ukraine and Crimea were communal pits of Gypsies and Jews. Gypsies were shot in the Jewish cemeteries at Oszmiany and left to starve to death in the Luzin synagogue.[20]

On the other hand, treatment of the Rom was not consistent throughout Russia. In parts of the Crimea, all nonmigratory Gypsies were ordered to be spared if they could prove that they had been living for two years in the roundup area.[21]

During the third wave of Gypsy incarceration in the Balkans, Rumanian and Hungarian Gypsies (as well as some from Austria) were brought to the Lodz ghetto in Poland. Although very little information has been recovered about the inhabitants sealed off in the "Gypsy Camp" in Lodz, names such as Horvath, Rigo, Papay, Retter, Fels, and Sarkozy were registered on lists of confiscated valuables. From November 5 to 9, 1941, five transports from five transient camps in the occupied territories of Austria arrived. Witnesses in the Jewish sector of Lodz who watched the arriving transports took these people to be Gypsy families as there were both male and female Gypsies dressed in typical Gypsy clothing. Along with the adults were a large number of children.[22] These internees would soon be transported to another camp in Poland. (See chapters 4 and 5.)

As in Russia, treatment was not consistent for these Balkan Gypsies. In some parts of Rumania, Gypsies remained relatively free. Records also show that (as in Germany and Italy) some Romany males served in the Rumanian army and that several were captured by the Russians.[23] Czechoslovakia, which had been divided into five parts by the Nazis, also had varying treatments, depending on where the Gypsies were located. In sections of Bohemia and Moravia, for example, most Gypsies were held in concentration camps. In other areas, they had some freedom, although they were forbidden to leave their place of residence without permission from the police. After the establishment of the special Gypsy camp at Auschwitz, deportations increased. In fact, Gypsies from Bohemia and Moravia (nearly 4,000) comprised the second largest group at the camp.[24]

Like Gypsies from Western Europe, many Rom would not have the "luxury" of an internment camp. They were killed immediately after being rounded up. Witnesses and survivors tell of mass slaughter at the hands of German troops, civilians, and Fascist militia. In Croatia, the Ustashi (members of a movement that had formed at the end of World War I to protest the union of Serbia and Croatia) "engaged in a bloodbath directed at Serbs,

Gypsies, and Jews."[34] Many times the Ustashi used primitive implements in putting their victims to death, including knives, axes, hammers, and other iron tools. Another method of killing was by binding pairs of prisoners back to back and then tossing them into the Save River to drown.[1]

A further example of the atrocities committed by the Ustashi was related by Angela Hudorovic and concerned the death of her sister and niece. Hudorovic stated that her niece was forced to dig a ditch while the girls' mother, who was seven months pregnant, was tied to a tree. "With a knife they opened the belly of the mother, took out the baby and threw it in the ditch…threw in the mother and the girl, after raping her…covered them with earth while they were still alive."[2] One source estimates that 40,000 Gypsies were killed by the Ustashis upon roundup or after being interned in Jasenovac camp.[3]

Mass executions of Gypsies in Serbia were also carried out by troops in the regular German Army. At times, Gypsies as well as Jews who were held hostage were shot by the army. A "Public Announcement" document mimeographed by partisans gives a list of individuals who were sentenced to death and shot as enemies of the Slovenian people. The names were listed as: Polde, Stane, and Natse Brajdich—Gypsies.[4]

Large-scale massacres outside of camps of both Jews and Gypsies began in Yugoslavia in October 1941, and both groups were also often killed as hostages. One hundred Jews and Gypsies were shot for each German soldier killed by patriots or guerrillas. Inhabitants around Belgrade also told of hearing the cries of children coming from trucks that were carrying them to be executed. A German lieutenant indicated that it was "easier to kill Jews than Gypsies, because they were quieter facing death than the Gypsies were."[5]

TEMPORARY EVASION

Whether through luck or resourcefulness, some Gypsies were able to elude the dragnets for a period of time in both Germany and the occupied countries or to make one or more escapes from various concentration camps and ghettos. Primo Levy writes of a bunkmate—a Gypsy named Grigo, who had been born in Spain and who had wandered about the countryside in Germany, Austria, and the Balkans. Whether he was more clever than many Gypsies, more opportunistic, or just plain lucky, he was able to evade imprisonment for several years. Finally, the nineteen-year-old Grigo had been captured in Hungary and interned in Auschwitz.[6]

Roman Mirga told of his family eluding capture by wandering and hiding for months with other Gypsies. Unfortunately, early on a spring morning in 1944, the group eventually encountered German soldiers in Hungary, near the Austrian border. The caravan was recognized as Sinti by the German colonel heading the troops. He directed the group to get their caravans and horses out of the way. When the Gypsies were slow in doing this, he ordered the wagons pushed into the ditch by the roadside. Ignoring the pleas of both Gypsy men and women, the colonel expressed his sorrow "for the horses" but had them and the caravan's dogs shot. When his aide asked what the soldiers were to do with the people, the colonel replied, "Get them into the half-empty trucks at the back of the column. Drive them across the border and hand them over to the commander of the nearest railway station. He will send them where they belong."[7]

The days of relative freedom for Mirga and his family were at an end.

> We were loaded like sacks of potatoes, thrown together with hardly space to breathe, twenty-five to each truck.... My whole body ached as if it had been beaten by rods...my mother's face contorted in agony...men paralysed with fear...children, clinging to their mothers' bodies, cried desperately.[8]

Mirga recalled that as the trucks drove them to the railway station, people stared at them, and a German staff officer had his car stopped so that he could take a photograph of the Gypsies. What the group ended up with were rail accommodations—Nazi style.

> We were herded together like cattle, standing because there was just room enough for old people to sit on the floor. We exchanged places at the ventilation slats frequently in order to share a whiff of fresh air and a glimpse of the outside world.[9]

In the afternoon black bread was tossed into the Gypsies but no water. Finally, Mirga's father took off his hat and asked a guard to fill it with water for those in the car. The next day the Gypsy car was disengaged from the engine and attached to another train consisting of five cattle cars. As Mirga peered out he managed to see signs with Stars of David and the word *Juden* on them. The Gypsies were going wherever the Jews were headed.[10]

Katja H.[11] and her family were also able to temporarily elude the trap in which most Gypsies were snared. She recalled that her grandfather had been more aware of what was happening in Bavaria than either his Gypsy or Jewish neighbors. Because of his decision to get his family out of Munich in 1939, and his wealth which permitted him to do so, his family would remain outside of the camps until 1944.

> My grandfather was not as foolish as some of the others. I can remember him saying to a Jewish friend, "Aren't you worried about what is going on?" Grandfather was a very rich man. He had a business and much gold. He was also, how do you say it—a forger. He forged papers for all of us to get out of Germany. First we went to Italy, in 1939, where we stayed for quite a while. I was nine years old at the time.

In Italy, Katja's grandparents, mother, father, uncle, aunt, and numerous cousins lived obscurely, mingling when the need arose with the Italian population.

> The Italians had dark skin like us, so we fit in nicely. We had gold, so it was easy for us to buy what we needed. But we kids didn't make friends with the Italian kids. We were told to stay away from the others, to play together with our own kind, to keep out of trouble where it might be discovered that we weren't really Italians.
>
> When the German troops became so thick in Italy as part of their alliance with Germany, and later, as we heard rumors of the Germans losing out in North Africa, my grandfather felt it was better if we left the country before our true identity could be discovered.

The family of Katja H. went by train to Rumania and then to Hungary, remaining for a period of months in each country—always fearful, always in hiding.

> We were scared many times—perhaps most of the time. People we would meet or stay with would tell us they were our friends and would hide us; then they would realize that they could get favors from the Germans for turning us in. We were always on the move. We were afraid to trust anyone.

Finally, Katja's family ended up in Yugoslavia. Their gold and money had not outlasted the Nazi regime, and they were taken in by a band of partisans. During a battle between the partisans and some German troops, the family was taken prisoner and shipped to a labor camp at Marburg in Germany. It had been a long game of hide-and-seek, but Katja's days of comparative freedom were at an end.

Unlike Katja's family, many Gypsies in Italy either did not have the financial means or the foresight to elude or postpone their capture. Francesco "Frank" P.,[12] an Italian citizen, remembered seeing Gypsy families rounded up by the Germans for transport to camps outside of Italy. Although Frank had served in the navy during the early years of the war, in late September 1943, along with other Italians, he was shipped in boxcars to Stuttgart, Germany, for forced labor in a German factory. Frank particularly recalled the harsh treatment of the workers by the SS troops and indicated that recalling that period of time in his life still causes him emotional problems.[13]

An almost unbelievable story is that of one Gypsy man who was able to ride out the entire war at the multinational civilian internment camp of Ilag VIII-Z near Kreutzberg in Upper Silesia. He was discovered by Henry Soderberg, a neutral Swede and a representative of the international YMCA, who was one of seven foreigners permitted to travel freely around Europe and to talk with German prisoners. When Soderberg arrived at Ilag VIII-Z in late December 1944, he found among the group of Greeks, Jews, Palestinians, Poles, and Czechs (who for one reason or another could claim British citizenship) the lone Gypsy. The man, name unknown, had been born in Glasgow, Scotland, and reared near Berlin. He had been wise enough to secure a British passport before the outbreak of war. Soderberg records in his diary that the Gypsy "could not speak a word of English, but the passport kept him out of the gas chamber."[14]

A few Gypsies were also able to survive outside the camps due to help from local populations. In one instance, a group of Gypsies stayed in the village of Talmina for quite some time as the authorities there issued them Italian identity cards. Having these cards placed the Gypsies beyond the reach of the Germans. While Gypsies were being exterminated in the camps of central Poland, as late as 1944, those in Eastern Galicia were permitted a good deal of freedom and allowed to engage in their tradi-tional trades.[15]

There were also examples of some Gypsy families being released, unaccountably, by the Nazis. One transport of Gypsies from south Ger-many was simply unloaded in Poland in the open country and told to fend for themselves. Some Gypsies sent to Poland were told by the Germans that they would be sterilized and sent to concentration camps if they returned to their homeland, and they had to sign documents to this effect.[16] This would seem to indicate that, although deported from their homes, they were fairly free to roam the Polish countryside. (It must be noted, though, that examples of release and/or sympathetic treatment from the Nazis or local populations in occupied countries were rare; most countries used the war as an excuse to rid themselves of all unwanted minorities—Gypsies, Jews, homosexuals, and so forth.)

Just as a few Gypsies were able to elude capture for periods of time or were sometimes released by their captors, some Gypsies escaped from the various internment areas. Of course, some individuals were more success-ful than others. José Santiago, who was in a forced labor squad at Romain-ville, France, escaped and made his way to Amiens. When he was arrested by the French police and asked why he was not doing compulsory labor ser-vice, Santiago "gave a story which somehow persuaded them to release him and make his way to the Vichy zone, remaining there undetected."[17]

Like José Santiago, Pollo R. made several escapes, although he was unable to retain his freedom for longer than a few months at a time. While interned in Poland at the holding area near Platerowa, he realized that security was lax during the workday as most guards were with the adult Gypsy laborers. Although the younger Gypsies had work to perform, they were not under constant supervision. One morning he found a way to slip into the woods and was soon on his way back to his native city of Krefeld and his grandparents' home. He might have made the journey successfully if he had not taken with him his eight-year-old sister. Pollo had made the mistake of sharing his plans with her, and she threatened to tell their par-ents if she were left behind. The exhausting journey by foot, the lack of almost any food for days at a time, the trouble finding shelter as winter set in, and the tension from fear of discovery were very difficult for the little girl. Her brother—himself only a young boy—did what he could to care for and protect her.

> We traveled mostly by night; during the day we hid in the trees or a haystack. We would go to the doors of Polish farmers because I could speak some Polish and ask for food. Sometimes a family would feel sorry for us and give us food and let us sleep in the stables. Other times, we were chased away for the families may have been afraid of what would happen to them if the Germans found out they had fed us. Or maybe like most they did not like Gypsies. We were always petrified of being discovered by German soldiers. We were forever hungry and wet or cold.

Still, the two children were able to make their way undetected as far as Rosenberg in what was then known as Prussia. There, unfortunately, they were seen and stopped by a Wehrmacht major who wondered why two small children were wandering alone about the countryside. When Pollo began answering questions in German, the major became even more suspicious because the complexion of the two was much darker than the typical German. Of course, Pollo had a "cover story" ready and explained that he and his sister were "ethnic" Germans who had been living in Russia. The Russians had killed their parents months earlier, he explained, and they were trying to reach Krefeld where their grandfather lived. However, the major was skeptical of Pollo's excuse and turned the two transients over to the authorities in Rosenberg.

> Because of the major we were placed in an orphanage in Rosenberg. Maybe he took pity on us because we were strays. Maybe he had children of his own at home. At any rate, the major wrote to our grandfather about our parents' death. Papo [the grandfather] had heard from our parents only days before and knew they were not dead. He immediately wrote back, stating that I had lied and that our parents were alive and living in Poland.
>
> But the people who ran the orphanage apparently felt sorry for us since it was so close to Christmas. They let us stay there through the holidays and then sent us back to Poland. I still remember a Christmas carol that was sung repeatedly while we were in the orphanage. It brings tears to my eyes today—fifty years later.

Pollo's grandfather was still free and living in his home in Krefeld and, like many other Europeans, was unaware of the extent of the internments or of the horror that would ultimately await his grandchildren. He merely assumed the two had run away from their new home—the resettlement camp in Platerowa. He probably felt that their parents would be terribly worried about their welfare; therefore, he had the Germans return the children to them.

So, although Pollo ended up back in Poland, he was always attuned to possible ways out of his predicament. On one other occasion he was able to make a temporary escape because he was fairly fluent in Polish. When the family was moved to Krakow, he learned that the Nazis were conscripting Polish men for forced farm labor in Germany and were seeking translators who could speak both Polish and German. Although only thirteen years old, and probably because translators were in scarce supply, Pollo was accepted as a German-speaking Pole. Soon he was transported with the other men back into Germany where he was able to remain for a couple of months.

Because of his swarthy complexion, raven-colored hair, and black eyes, Pollo may have been suspect. However, he called attention to himself only when he got into a fight with a Gestapo man who had come to the farm where Pollo was working and wanted to appropriate a pig. Pollo indicated that he was responsible for the animals and could not give permission for the removal of the pig. When the man persisted in his request, Pollo emphasized his "No" by brandishing a pitchfork at the man. The man left but returned shortly with the farm supervisor. Immediately, Pollo was sent back to Poland—this time to Auschwitz-Birkenau.

Much like Pollo and his little sister, the Reinhardts were able to make an escape. The parents, three girls, and three boys had been put on a train from Hohenasberg bound for Poland. When the train stopped at night for track switching, the father was somehow able to get his family off and into the dark forests of Poland. The Reinhardts remained free for two years by avoiding cities and highways—begging food, sleeping wherever they found shelter, sometimes earning a little money playing violins and guitars at small country weddings in out-of-the-way villages where there was less of a chance of discovery by the authorities. Eventually, the Nazis caught up with them and they were imprisoned.[18] (After the war, one of the boys,

Janko Reinhardt, migrated to the United States where he became a jazz guitarist.)

These few examples of evasion and escape tend to show that the Nazis could not capture and kill every Gypsy, yet for hundreds of thousands, immediate death would be their fate. For most other Romany families years of imprisonment and eventual death would be in their future. Like other prisoners, the Gypsies would soon realize that the quality of their day-to-day existence in the various internment camps and their chances for remaining alive until the end of the war depended upon several factors—the particular camp they were sent to, the needs of the Third Reich for captive labor, the personality and whims of their captors, and their own survival skills.

Four

❧

The Effort of Survival

The Gypsies were all undernourished. I controlled and tasted the food in the kitchen. It was a sort of grain soup, no, rather it was a water soup with a few grains swimming in it. The imprisoned Gypsies were often shrunken to skeletons.... I wrote a memo immediately but Hartjenstein (commander of Birkenau) said, "Oh, they're only Gypsies after all."
—Donald Kenrick and Grattan Puxon,
The Destiny of Europe's Gypsies

FOR THOSE WHO WERE interned, the term "concentration camp" is much too vague. Nor is the term "survival" precise enough to demonstrate the day-to-day life of camp inmates. Survival meant enduring the loss of all privacy and dignity. Survival meant tolerating the pervasive stench of vomit, urine, and feces. Survival meant outlasting the biting cold, constant hunger, and random beatings. Survival meant ignoring the cries and moans that permeated the darkness. Survival meant cheating death for a few days, a few months, or a few years. Indeed, *survival* meant only a postponement of death.

Each camp, during its years of existence, would take on a different makeup, depending on its location and the personality of those in control. Certain camps or their satellites would be designated for Jews, or Gypsies or other "asocials"; however, intermingling often occurred regardless of race, religion, ethnic background, or political bent. Although treatment in all of the camps was generally brutish, occasionally somewhat milder conditions could exist. For example, being a Gypsy in a French camp could mean a relative degree of freedom where internees were permitted to leave the compound and work in town for a few days each month. On the other hand, being interned in Poland or in most other camps scattered across Europe could mean endless days of backbreaking labor dredging ditches to drain the surrounding swampy ground, quarrying rock, or digging pits in frozen ground to accommodate an ever-increasing number of corpses.

Regardless of the circumstances, for most, existence was a never-ending struggle.

Survival was most elusive at the infamous Auschwitz—known to most as *Vernichtungslager*, the annihilation camp. Separated only by a strand of barbed wire was the satellite camp of Birkenau, a part of which was known as the "family camp" of the Gypsies. In his memoirs Commandant Rudolph Höss indicated that he could not recall how many Gypsies were in the camp but that "they completely filled the section of the camp designed for ten thousand prisoners." (The Auschwitz Museum reports that a total of 20,943 Gypsies were inmates.)[1]

Although conditions in Birkenau were deplorable with poor hygienic conditions, poor nourishment, and high death rates from illness (and eventually all of the Gypsies remaining in the camp would be exterminated), surviving members of Gypsy families were allowed to be in close proximity to each other for some periods of time. Why this was done is unclear, but perhaps it explains reports that Gypsies appeared to be "more content" than other prisoners. While they were separated into men's barracks and women's barracks, they at least had the nearness of loved ones to offer some meager bit of physical and emotional support.

For young Pollo, this turned out to be the case when, for several months before being shipped to another camp, he was reunited with his family at Auschwitz. Wandering among strangers as he tried to become acclimated to the Gypsy camp, Pollo was startled to feel a hand on his shoulder. Turning around, he stared into intense black eyes.

> Father, is that you? I cried. I couldn't believe what I was seeing. I was shrieking hysterically. "Yes, it's me, or rather what's left of me," he replied. While we were still hugging and kissing, a hand went over my head. I knew only one person who touched me like this. Mother! I flew into her arms. Then I felt a tugging on my jacket and saw that my little brothers and sisters were also there. It was unbelievable to find them like this.
>
> Tears of joy and anger ran down my face. Everybody was bald; even father's pride, his moustache, had been shaved off. Everybody appeared to be held together by their skin only. My mother had changed greatly. Her fiery eyes had become dim, the spring in her walk had given way to a drag, and she was so very thin. Always somehow

figuring out what I was thinking, she said, "We don't get much to eat here, a thin slice of bread in the mornings, and if you work, half a liter of broth, made up of rotten turnips, for lunch. Even the little ones. But so far it has kept us alive."

Pollo's family were quick to point out to him that, as they could not provide much food, they also could not physically protect him from the guards. He was warned that breaking the rules could mean death. "If you need to go tonight, use the bed pan or the bucket in the corner," Father warned me. "Don't go outside; we have curfew from 8:00 P.M. until 5:00 A.M. If the guards see you outside the barracks, you'll be shot on the spot." Still, although the suffering in Auschwitz-Birkenau was continuous, the fact that members of Pollo's family could maintain some contact with each other made their wretched existence more bearable.

However, as with other prisoners, most Gypsy families were torn apart and dispersed throughout the concentration camp system. Often they were shuffled from one camp to another. For example, Asta F. (who died in 1990) was moved first to Ohrdruf, then to Theresienstadt, to Ravensbrück, to Mauthausen (in Austria), and then back all the way across Germany to Bergen-Belsen. While at Ravensbrück, Asta learned that a new transport of Gypsies had been brought from Auschwitz-Birkenau. Asta crept out of her block (barracks) and into the quarantine block to see if she could find any of her younger brothers or sisters among the new arrivals.

I looked and looked to see if I would see someone in my family. I was sniffling at the thought that I would not find anyone. I was not being very careful to not be seen. Just then one of the guards came up behind me and hit me across the mouth with the end of his rifle for being outside my barracks. I remember I couldn't eat for several days as my mouth was so badly cut and bruised. It was so swollen that my whole face looked different.

Three days later as she was walking around the compound, Asta saw a man whom she thought she recognized as her father.

But this man was bald and had no moustache. The last time I had seen my father, he had a full head of black hair and a huge black moustache. I begged the woman guard on my knees, "Please, please let me speak to that man. I think he's my father but I haven't seen him in three years." She was one of the good ones. She let me approach. It was my father. I said, "Tatta," and he recognized me by my voice. My face was still disfigured from being beaten by the guard. He cried at seeing me in such a state, but I didn't want to cry and upset him more. So I smiled outside, but my heart was crying.

Asta's father asked if she was getting anything to eat, and she told him that there was plenty of food and she was doing very well. "I tried to comfort him, so I had to lie about the food. I could see that he was very upset at my appearance, and I didn't want to worry him further. All I wanted was that he was content and not to worry. It was such a little lie about the food, but he seemed to accept it."

IMMINENT STARVATION

Like that of other prisoners in the camps, the Gypsies' days consisted of a never-ending struggle to find food, fight disease, keep warm, and gather the strength to meet the heavy work schedules imposed by their captors. The most insidious and constant enemy of all was hunger—nagging, unrelieved hunger. Almost no food was available, particularly as the war continued into its fifth and sixth year. No matter who they were or where they were imprisoned, the diet of adult victims provided just enough calories to keep them functioning. Seven hundred calories a day for adults was often the rule with less for children. Some parents gave their rations to their children; often the prisoners fought each other for scraps of food. Survivors' memories are dominated by their perpetual craving for almost any form of sustenance. There was never enough, and what was allotted to the prisoners was many times inedible—scraps of rancid meat, watery soup, and moldy bread made from weevil-filled flour. Access to rotting garbage could be a luxury. Some chewed splinters of wood or nibbled small amounts of dirt to help fill their stomachs. Steadily, all lost weight.

Gypsy Mateo Maximoff recalled that while in the French prison camp called Gurs, over a two-year period his weight dropped from approximately 165 pounds to just 97 pounds.

> Many of us died. To earn one bowl of soup we had to gather a truckload of wood. I have seen a Gypsy carry out the garbage, and then fight other prisoners with his pocketknife for a rotting fish head.[2]

Still, Maximoff believed that the French camps were not as bad as the camps in Germany or those under German auspices.

To obtain food for themselves or to pass on to their loved ones, the Gypsies used any method available. Pollo R. had devised a rather unique scheme for getting food while in the internment camp Dora, a satellite of Buchenwald. One of his duties was to feed the pigs which would later be butchered for the SS officers' mess. Although the pig stall was only about a half mile from the SS kitchen, he was always given an armed escort as he toted the pails of leftover food from the officers' mess. Because these leftovers used to fatten the pigs were considerably better than the daily food rations of the prisoners, the other inmates would have attacked Pollo for the swill were it not for his guards.

However, Pollo was not above eating the garbage himself and soon formulated an undetected method of sharing the pigs' meal.

> What was garbage to the SS was a delicacy to us starving prisoners. Because only the best leftovers were granted to the pigs, not to us, I had trained the pigs very well. After I had poured the food into the trough, the SS guard would leave me. But the pigs would *not* start eating before I finished eating out of their trough. On previous encounters when we all—the pigs and me—were sticking our heads into the trough, I would get bumped around by the fairly heavy pigs. But I began to bite their ears and snouts until they got the point and did not approach their food until I had my fill. This additional food helped keep me alive and able to do my assigned work.

When possible, and if he could find some kind of container, Pollo would smuggle garbage to his blockmates. On one occasion he was able to get quite a large amount of pork for several of the other starving men. During his usual pig-feeding time, and after the guard had returned to his office, Pollo beat one pig so severely that it had red streaks all over its body. Then he called the SS guard back to the sty and convinced him that the pig was suffering from a dangerous, contagious disease. The guard shot the pig and told Pollo and several other prisoners to bury it in lime as it was contagious. "Later that day, in an unobserved moment, we dug the pig back out of its lime grave and ate it. We scraped as much of the lime off as we could, but we were determined not to let a morsel go to waste; it's a wonder we didn't all die."

When she was in Bergen Belsen, Wanda G. was severely beaten with the stock of a guard's rifle as she attempted to steal a rotten beet from off a garbage heap.

> It was for my little sister. She was so weak from lack of food. She was whimpering from hunger pains—day after day. Finally, she just lay in her bunk. I thought she would die if I couldn't get her some kind of food. So I was beaten for nothing as I didn't get the beet.

For as long as her health permitted, Asta F. always asked to work extra shifts in the Ravensbrück kitchen.

> The food we were provided with was nothing—soup without any base, just water with whatever was available thrown in. Some lard or grease, cabbage and potatoes, if we could get them. But not enough of anything solid or nourishing to chew on. But we had salt and it was hot. There was usually some kind of bread, many times hard as a rock, many times covered with spots of blue mold, but we dipped in. We survived.

By working after her shift was over and helping clean up the kitchen area, Asta was in a better position to steal any leftover scraps of food for her younger sisters who were unable to fend for themselves. In addition, during the winter months, the stoves from the kitchen provided welcome relief from the harsh weather.

THE THREAT OF DISEASE

Starvation contributed significantly to another major enemy of the inmates—disease. It lurked among the cold, emaciated, and overworked prisoners like the specter of death. At Auschwitz-Birkenau, disease eliminated many Gypsies before they could be shot or gassed. Many of the barracks had open holes without doors; hygienic conditions were deplorable. "It was a bog with horse stables without windows.... The people waded up to their ankles in slime."[3] Although the camps had hospitals, medical care for the inmates was nonexistent. Roman Mirga recalled that he often saw in the hospital Gypsies "dying by hundreds every day" of spotted fever, scarlet fever, smallpox, dysentery, typhoid, and tuberculosis.[4]

Commandant Höss commented about the cancerlike illness called "noma" which he compared to leprosy as it rotted the skin and which left huge holes in the cheeks of the Gypsy children. According to Höss the death rate among Gypsy children in Birkenau was "exceptionally high. I do not believe that many of the newborns survived the first weeks."[5]

In Lodz, 5,000 Gypsies from Burgenland, Austria, arrived in November 1941. One source indicates that almost from the moment of their arrival "terrible cries and screams could be heard.... Every evening...cars crammed with drunken Germans [were] going into the Gypsy camp. All windows had been smashed there—this at the peak of the winter frosts."[6]

Kept separated by barbed wire from the Jewish ghetto at Lodz, the Gypsies had to be supplied with both food and medical assistance by the ghetto Jews. Shortly after their arrival, spotted typhus began to spread through the Gypsy population. In one of the most detailed accounts of life in the Lodz ghetto, Jewish writers record their orders from the German criminal police to take charge of caring for the ill Gypsies and interring their dead.

As the typhus epidemic continued through December and into January 1942, several German doctors who had been attending the ill Gypsies contracted the disease and died. As a result, all Jewish doctors up to the age of forty-five were then delegated to work in the Gypsy camp through a system of drawing lots.[7] Records from the Jews in Lodz gives some idea of the number of dead, whether they were adults or children, and the methods of burial.

> As of today (December 1, 1941), the Department of Burials has buried 213 people.... In accordance with the orders...the Department of Burials is obliged to send a hearse to the grounds of the Gypsy camp every day no later than 9:00 A.M. Since there are frequently many bodies...the hearses now arrive at the camp by six o'clock in the morning.
>
> In the beginning...the overwhelming majority of the bodies removed from the camp were those of children. It was only toward the end of last month that there were more adults than children being buried.[8]

An isolated section of the Jewish cemetery had been set aside prior to the war for burial of any Gypsies who were originally residents of Lodz or the nearby vicinity. This same area was utilized for interments from the Gypsy camp. Unfortunately, the identity of the dead Gypsies would not be known for the Department of Burials received no personal data on the corpses.

> The bodies are received without clothing and, most frequently, are in their underclothing.... [W]hen it is necessary to bury a greater number of bodies, the cemetery carpenters are, for technical reasons, unable to prepare a sufficient number of covered boxes to serve as coffins. In those cases the bodies are buried on planks.[9]

Apparently hundreds of Gypsies succumbed to the spotted typhus in Lodz while the remainder were quickly trucked to the concentration camp at Chelmno. However, again a discrepancy in reporting exists. Some records indicate that many of the Gypsies in Lodz were "exterminated" before they could die of disease. (See chapter 5.)

Lena Winterstein's mother was one of the thousands to become seriously ill while in one of the Polish camps. She was taken to what Winterstein implies was some sort of hospital or place where medical care was available. "Three days later, when I was going to visit her, I was told she had died." Winterstein stated that for a long time she was bothered with dreams that her mother was in some sort of crate, barely covered, just dumped in the ground.[10]

While he was confined in Dora in late 1944, Pollo R. became ill with tuberculosis and was told to report to "sick call" at the camp hospital. However, Pollo was now about sixteen years old and after years in the camp system, he knew that going to the hospital was similar to "signing your own death certificate." So he did nothing, preferring to wait and hope that his illness would not prevent him from reporting for labor details. "I knew that if I could keep at work, no one would be at all concerned about whether I was ill or not. You did not want to have the Germans learn that you were ill or it would all be over."

FORCED LABOR

Another partner in the impossible odds facing the internees was the long days of strenuous work with no respite from the blazing heat of summer or the bitter cold of winter. This arduous labor drained the camp inmates of the little life they had left. Prisoners were up at 5 A.M. in the summer and

6 A.M. in the winter. Work was a minimum of twelve hours a day, seven days a week. There were no holidays.

Wanda G. remembered working one day cleaning a sewage pit near her block. Two other inmates working with her asked if she knew it was Christmas Day. When she replied that she did not know what day it was, they said, "Well, we know, because earlier Commandant Höss was riding around camp on his horse announcing that anyone who gets beaten to death today—Christmas—will get a candle stuck up his ass in lieu of a candle put on a Christmas tree."

Because the Germans strove to maintain wartime production, virtually everybody had to work, with the exception of very small children up to two years old. Even children between the ages of three and nine had "little jobs" to perform under the supervision of a children's supervisor who was appointed by the camp commandant. The older children were already in the regular working parties with the adults.[11] On a starvation diet, only a few survived for very long; many were worked to death.

BRUTALITY

As if starvation, disease, and overwork weren't enough, the sadistic treatment by their captors also detracted from the Gypsies' chances of survival. Repeated brutality by the guards and Kapos severely complicated life for the Gypsies. Beatings and torture would leave many physically and emotionally damaged for life. The blows from a guard's rifle fractured Wanda G.'s skull and knocked her senseless as she attempted to steal some bits of food. She lay on the ground motionless, and the fact that she appeared dead may have saved her from further harm. With the help of several other inmates, Wanda's mother carried her inside their blockhouse. No medical help was available so the mother used some herbs gathered in the woods surrounding the camp to eventually nurse her child back to health; however, from then on Wanda suffered from epileptic seizures.

One time Pollo R. was given the task of filling sacks with straw to be used as mattresses in the blocks. Near the end of the workday, he had completed his chore and since the guards were nowhere near his area, he lay down on the sacks to rest for just a few moments.

I had fallen asleep. I didn't notice that it was inspection time and slept through the inspection. They looked for me all over the camp. I woke to hear blaring from the loudspeaker, "Inmate 41916 to the gate immediately in a running gait." I think they thought that somehow I had been able to make an escape.

I couldn't get out because I was locked in the work shed. I kept on hearing the announcement over the speaker, and I knew that as long as someone was missing the entire camp had to stand in formation—even if it had taken ten hours to find the one that was missing.

I knocked on the door and yelled as loudly as I could, but they didn't hear me. They formed a search command made up of Kapos and camp police, and they eventually found me. Then I had to run all the way down to the gate. It was a very long distance, and I did not have my full strength. When I reached the gate, I was badly beaten with the stock of a rifle.

In addition to the beating, and without being given any medical attention for his welts and bruises, Pollo was required to stand at attention at the front gate for twenty-four hours. "It was bitterly cold, and I thought I would freeze my feet off. But I couldn't move about to help circulate the blood; I was required to stand still."

Asta F. recalled the severe beating her mother received. Along with several other Gypsy parents Asta's mother had signed a permission form for the sterilization of her daughters. She had been told by the camp administration that if she would allow the sterilization, her two daughters would be released from camp. Believing what she was told, she signed. Later, when the girls were not released from the camp, Asta's mother questioned why her daughters were still being detained. For daring to question the camp authorities, "My mother was given twenty-five lashes with a whip. There were huge welts all over her body. She was hardly able to walk for several days. Some of the other adults helped care for her as, of course, there was no medical aid from the Germans."[12]

Some prisoners, of course, would not survive the physical abuse. One Gypsy who was attempting to escape from Dachau was locked in a box with iron bars blocking the opening. The box was so small that the prisoner could not stand up but had to stay in a crouching position.

Koch (the camp commander) then had big nails driven through the planks so that each movement of the prisoner made them stick in his body. Without food or water, he spent two days and three nights in this position. On the morning of the third day, having already gone insane, he was given an injection of poison.[13]

Although the above accounts are appalling, and it makes one wonder how any Gypsies endured these years of wretched living conditions, some were able to outlast their brutal treatment. Many, however, were already or would become a part of the "Gypsy genocide," indiscriminately destroyed by the hundreds of thousands—tortured to death in experiments, shot in isolated areas, and suffocated in gas chambers.

Five

Gypsy Genocide

On the back wall is a shack built, which he opens. It's a morgue. I have seen many corpses in the concentration camp, but here I am grabbed by horror. A mound of corpses, a good seven feet high. Almost all children, babies and juveniles, over them hastily the rats fleeting.
—Hermann Langbein, in the Gypsy Camp at Auschwitz

{ONGINGLY I LOOKED AT the gate which barred my way out of the compound filled with screaming humanity. Near me on several trucks were hundreds of nude men, women, and children. Although they had not been on my transport, like me they were Gypsies, only they were from Silesia," Pollo R. recalled.

I could hear and understand their prayers in Romany. They implored God (but in vain) to spare at least their children's lives. I was only fourteen at the time, and now realize that I had no real understanding of the situation I was witnessing. But instinctively I knew that something unimaginable was going to happen!

We were told to line up quickly. Those that lagged were hit with batons. One SS guard barked at us as he pointed toward the chimney stacks which seemed to reach for the sky like long, threatening fingers, "This will be *your* way out of Auschwitz!"

Thus Pollo R. explained his introduction to Auschwitz-Birkenau, the infamous Jewish/Gypsy camp. The section of Auschwitz-Birkenau where Gypsies would be confined began operation in March 1943 and ended operation in August 1944. Initially, the Gypsy camp, which consisted of thirty-two poorly constructed barracks called "B II e" was located in a swampy area void of vegetation. Originally it was not fenced; however, in July 1943, electrical wire was used to isolate this section from the other parts of Birkenau. In this camp, many Gypsies, called by Commandant Rudolph

Höss his "favorite inmates,"[1] would lose their lives because of the calculated strategy of their captors to cleanse Europe of racial impurities.

How many Gypsies perished in mass exterminations, scattered as they were in the concentration camps across Europe, is unclear. Because of the haphazard methods used to capture and slaughter the Gypsies, the rumors that abounded, and the contrasting recollections from eyewitnesses or survivors, the numbers vary greatly with the sources reporting. To the Nazis, Gypsy prisoners were most of the time considered "not important." Therefore death reports are usually compiled from verbal sources and their accuracy is questionable. Often Gypsy families were killed in their entirety, leaving no survivors to report on the number of murdered relatives.

In Auschwitz, where there tended to be *official* registration, records indicate 20,943 died or were killed; however, even here discrepancies appear. Dr. Robert Ritter (director of the Section for Research on Race-hygiene and Population Biology in the Reich Department of Health, Berlin) mentioned the figure 23,822 "Gypsy cases" in the camp, a number 14 per cent higher than registered. (No explanation is given for the inconsistency in the head-count.) It is known that the Gypsies of East Prussia, who arrived late in March 1943, were sent immediately to the Auschwitz gas chambers, apparently without being registered.[2] Some reports indicate that usually Gypsies from the Balkans also were killed as soon as they reached the camps.

In addition, of the 20,943 Gypsies registered in Auschwitz, between 2,000 and 3,461 were sent to other camps, where their fate remains unknown. Eventually the Gypsy camp ceased to exist as a separate entity, for "[a]fter 2,897 children, women, and men (including former soldiers of the Wehrmacht) were driven into the gas chambers on the night of 2–3 August 1944, there were no more Gypsies left in Auschwitz."[3]

Some scholars of the holocaust believe that between a fourth and a third of all Gypsies living in Europe were killed by the Nazis. Simon Wiesenthal, the noted hunter of holocaust perpetrators, wrote that "the Gypsies had been murdered [in a proportion] similar to the Jews; about 80% of them in the area of the countries which were occupied by the Nazis."[4] The mechanism of the Final Solution, which had been set up to eliminate Jews, eventually was used to eliminate most of Europe's Gypsies.

Auschwitz

What Pollo R. had so desperately been avoiding during his months in Germany as a translator finally caught up with him in Auschwitz, as it would catch up with so many millions of Jews, Gypsies, and other internees. He had survived the seemingly endless transport in the cattle car—the overpowering odors of excrement, urine, vomit, and decomposing bodies. One of two Gypsies (although Pollo had not previously known the other Gypsy) among 500 Jews, he had endured the crying of hungry and thirsty children and the gasps of the dying.

I had survived my time after being placed in the Radomsko ghetto (Poland). I was certain that things could not get worse for me. During the long train ride I had repeatedly assured myself that this was not happening. You are having a very bad dream, a nightmare. But I was not dreaming a nightmare. This time I would not be able to escape.

Now here we were, standing like a herd of frightened animals, trembling, many of the women and children sobbing, not knowing what to expect. My first breath of air outside the cattle car had brought me close to fainting. The air was filled with the stench of burned flesh. The smokestacks would be *my* way out of Auschwitz?

My mind echoed the SS guard's threat in disbelief. Surely he couldn't be serious. I reassured myself that he just wanted to scare us. I remembered how painful it was when I had once burned myself on the stove when I was much younger. I was trying to imagine how horrible it must be to be burned to death.... I thought of my mother, my father, my sister Mia; I wondered where they or others of my family were.

Besides the armed SS guards Pollo stated that the "welcoming committee" that day at Auschwitz consisted of Obersturmführer Mengele, the camp's commandant, Hauptsturmführer Schwarzhuber, a Hauptscharführer Plagge, and an Oberscharführer Platisch. As the group was herded past these men, Mengele would make signs with his hand, pointing to the right or to the left. Pollo was directed to the left, although he did not learn until later that the reason for this was that he had come with the Jewish transport, destined for immediate extermination. He remembers that he began to be concerned when he saw children torn from their desperate mothers, who were led off to the right. "One mother threw herself protectively over her baby," Pollo stated. "An SS guard walked up to her and shot her in the neck; then he kicked away the dead mother of the crying infant and shot it in the head. Conditions had been bad in Radomsko but nothing like this. Now I began to realize that these men were not human beings; they were creatures without a heart, escaped from hell."

Shortly, Pollo and the other people who had been directed to the left of the welcoming committee were told to march towards a building where they would be permitted "to shower."

> A shower? What a luxury! God knows, I could use a shower; a drop of water had not touched my skin since I didn't know how long. Although, given a choice, I would have opted for something to eat instead. But who knows? Things might look different after a shower. I was given a bar of soap and told to remember the number of my peg where I was to hang my clothes. I remember I was very anxious and worried about forgetting my peg number and losing my clothes. Clothing was almost impossible to come by, and I knew that many would steal it if they could. I was very concerned about somebody taking mine.

Completely undressed, with a bar of soap in his hand, Pollo anticipated the upcoming shower as he slowly moved along with his fellow Gypsy and the remaining Jews.

"You are Gypsies, aren't you?" asked a man dressed in a striped suit, who Pollo would later learn was a Kapo (prisoners selected by the Germans to be in charge of other inmates).

"Yes, we are."

"Get dressed, then," the Kapo directed the two Gypsies. "It isn't your turn yet."

"But..." Confused, I started to argue, when he harshly cut me off.

"Keep quite. Just get dressed and come with me."

Not knowing what was going on, both Gypsies dressed hurriedly. The Kapo escorted them to the end of another long line of people and left, never saying another word. As he waited behind the others in line, Pollo's eyes began to water from the faintly sweet odor of scorched flesh. As he moved forward, he discovered its origin. He stared in disbelief. Surely the SS did not brand people like cattle. "I was very, very frightened; then I felt a touch on my shoulder."

When Pollo looked around his eyes met those of an older man. Gently the man said, "I know it will hurt; be strong; it all will pass."

"I calmed down," Pollo recollected, "but the stinging pain in my left forearm was nearly unbearable. The arm had begun to swell almost instantly and eventually would become infected and make me extremely ill. In spite of the swelling I could read a number and a letter on my lower left arm." Pollo R. was now number Z9024. Only in Auschwitz would the Gypsies be branded; the Z in front of the number stood for *Zigeuner*, the German word for Gypsy.[5] The meaning of this brand was unmistakable. It meant, "You will never leave here; this is the mark with which slaves are branded and cattle sent to the slaughter, and that is what you have become."[6]

What this young Gypsy boy had so far seen had become a routine way of life for the other Gypsies in camp. The transports into Auschwitz were never-ending—day and night victims arrived from all parts of Europe. Soon there were thousands of Gypsies in the camp, mostly from Czechoslovakia and Germany. However, the camp also consisted of Polish, Russian, Hungarian, Dutch, Norwegian and Lithuanian Gypsies. In the final days a small number even were shipped in from French concentration camps.[7]

Exterminations became commonplace. For example, in 1943, a large transport of Polish Gypsies had arrived by train and were separated from the other Gypsies into two blocks. At first these new arrivals were elated to find medical personnel at the camp who also spoke Polish. However, after only two or three weeks all were sent to the gas chambers under the pretext that the Germans were preventing a typhoid epidemic. The camp administration was keen on liquidating Polish Gypsies shortly after their arrival. During these liquidations, many hospitalized children were pulled from their beds and taken to be gassed.[8]

In late July 1944, an earlier decision by Himmler that the Gypsy camp must be destroyed was carried out. Apparently, as lorries drove into the camp, some Gypsies believed they were being taken to another camp. When they realized that their destination was the crematoria, many tried to resist but were beaten down with clubs and had dogs set loose upon them. The SS and other prisoners carried sick persons out of the hospital to the lorries. A few Gypsy children who had hidden or been hidden by their parents were pulled from the blocks, held by their feet, and smashed against block walls.[9] The sixteen months' life of the Gypsy Camp at Auschwitz came to an end, with only a very few Gypsies who had been sent to other camps surviving this time of horror.

Over the few months that the Gypsy camp was in existence, more than 20,000 Gypsies were murdered. The oldest was 110-year-old Hanna Tomaszewicz; the youngest was one-month-old Wiktoria Ditloff. Two lines from a Gypsy song about this extermination sum up the history of the "Gypsy camp."

> They took us in through the gate
> They let us out through chimneys[10]

It is interesting to note that the commander of Birkenau in 1944, Schwarzhuber, told Höss that killing the Gypsies had been more difficult for him than his involvement in the mass extermination of Jews. He indicated that it had been particularly hard on him as he knew many Gypsies individually and had been on good terms with them.[11]

Still, if one were given a choice, the gas chambers might have been the more humanitarian way of death. For many, torture in the form of medical experiments and slow, painful death would be their "way out of Auschwitz." Probably the best known of those who conducted experiments on prisoners is Dr. Mengele, although there were certainly others involved in experimentation. Mengele, who was at the camp for a "rest" after serving in the Ukraine and North Africa, took a special interest in Gypsy and Jewish twins. While records indicate that Mengele often played with Gypsy children, it is also recorded that "he shot a pair of twins in order to perform an autopsy on them." Moreover, Gypsy twins were separately killed, and Mengele would perform autopsies before the bodies were placed in the crematorium.[12]

One Jewish survivor of Auschwitz, who supervised fifty sets of Gypsy twins, described a pair whom Mengele had "sewn together, back to back, like Siamese twins." In agony from infected wounds oozing pus, they screamed constantly; finally their parents managed to obtain some morphine and, in order to end their suffering, killed them.[13]

On the other hand, one source states that there were a few Gypsy mothers, aware of Mengele's evil interests, who sent non-twin children as twins to Mengele.[14] Apparently, this was done chiefly because better food, clothing, and shelter were provided for twins; therefore the "fake" twins also could benefit from the improved conditions, at least temporarily.

A particularly vivid recollection of torturous death was given by Gypsy survivor Hans Braun of a Gypsy boy who had a long needle stuck into his back for the extraction of spinal fluid. When the needle broke and the child died, Mengele "cut the child open from the neck to the genitals, dissecting the body, and took out the innards to experiment on.[15] It is further recorded that some Gypsy children were beheaded, the heads then preserved in formaldehyde for use in German medical institutions.[16]

In the early 1940s, a group of 250 Gypsy children were taken from their parents in Brno, Czechoslovakia, and used in experiments to test the efficiency of the poison gas Cyklon B. While imprisoned in Dachau, Romany inmates were among those used to determine the amount of salt water an individual could drink before dying.[17]

Viktor Frankl observed that the continuous torture and death of children finally ceased to elicit much emotion from other prisoners. He recounts the incident of an internee watching a doctor pick off with tweezers the black, gangrenous stumps of a twelve-year-old boy's frozen toes. Having seen so much horror, the internee became merely a disinterested spectator.[18]

Like the children, adults were not exempt from the torture of experimentation and slow death. For pregnant women, camp life could be particularly trying. Pregnant Gypsy women (one witness testified to seeing eighty-six cases) were often infected with typhus bacteria so that the effect of the infection on the fetus could be determined.[19] Another man indicated that while he had become accustomed to seeing totally emaciated prisoners, he was appalled at the conditions of a "maternity ward." Here were Gypsy women who had recently given birth lying in a frigid ward, nude and without blankets. Most were in a stupor, unaware of their nudity. (For Gypsies nudity before others is endless shame.) There was one woman, singing quietly to herself. "She had lost her mind. She was the lucky one."[20]

There was no special food for the mothers and newborns and very little water. Immediately after a birth SS guards would see to it that a prisoner number was tattooed on the upper thigh of the infant. Of course, the infant mortality rate was extremely high, most newborn babies living only a few weeks. In one barracks where new mothers lay, prisoner Hermann

Langbien described the conditions: "The floor was of clay and at one end there was a curtain. There I saw a pile of children's bodies, and among them, rats."[21]

For the inmates at Auschwitz death was always among them. If they were ill and taken to the "sick barracks," seldom did they recover. Up to ten ill persons slept in bunks designed for four with water dripping from the ceiling onto their bodies. Many lay for days in their own excrement. Untrained Gypsies gave what little care was available. "Every day twenty to thirty died and their bodies were placed in one corner of the barrack and collected each evening by a special commando."[22]

Pollo came face to face with the large number of Gypsy deaths when he was awakened on his first night in the camp, and many subsequent nights, by the gruesome sounds of dead bodies being rolled out of bunks and onto the floor of his barracks. The next morning the bodies were collected and stacked neatly in a corner. As he stared in amazement at the apparent unconcern of those handling the bodies, his mother explained. "Child, I know what you are thinking, but while one never gets used to this, you have to ignore it to keep your sanity." Eventually, Pollo found that what she said was true.

> I don't know how long I had been in Auschwitz, but summer had given way to fall. While many of the prisoners had died of dehydration working in the hot sun, now we were faced with the harshness of the Polish winter. It was very cold now in the wooden barracks. We would huddle together at night in the Buxen (tiers of bunks) to keep our starved bodies warm.

> On one such night I woke up because I felt something ice cold in my back. I put my hand behind me to touch the source of the cold. In horror I realized that the person who had huddled onto me must have died some time ago, because rigor mortis had already begun to take hold of his body. I sat up, with my back to the wall, and with my feet rolled the body out of the Buxe, until he fell with a final thump to the floor. Mother had been right; one had to ignore the suffering that was going on in order to remain sane.

> Time and the cold of late fall was taking its toll. Every morning we had in our block twenty or thirty dead people strewn over the barrack floor. They had died during the night of starvation, typhoid, and merciless beatings. The first order of the day would be to throw the

dead bodies in a pile by the back door. Later in the day a twenty-five-ton truck would stop at each block and pick up their grim cargo which was then carried to the crematorium.

Twice Pollo nearly became one of these dead. He was severely beaten by Hauptsturmführer Plagge, after Pollo gave an unacceptable reply to Plagge's questions. Plagge first reached for his pistol but then caught sight of a spade leaning against the barracks wall. "He kicked me first in the back and hit me on the head. Then he knocked the spade apart so only the long handle remained in his hand. Ordering me to 'Lie down across the chimney,' he beat me until I was unconscious."

Even though he survived, Pollo could never forget his work with the dead. On a particular day he was ordered not to go to the drainage areas but to stay behind and help dig mass graves as the ovens were not working properly, and many of the bodies could not be cremated. "Up until that day I had been under the impression that the people had been cremated with their clothes on," Pollo stated. "My horrid task, after I had helped dig the pit, consisted of taking the prison garb off the partially decomposed bodies, throwing the bodies into the grave, and taking the suits to the laundry. I remember that a cold chill ran down my spine. I wondered who had died in my clothing before it became mine."

Amid all the horror in Auschwitz-Birkenau, the Gypsies still attempted to maintain some semblance of community. In fact, this was one aspect of the Gypsies that seemed to amaze Rudolph Höss—"Within their clans...they stuck together as if they were glued and they were very devoted to one another."[23]

Most tried to protect others who became ill and infirm, they taught the young Gypsies their language and customs, and they played their Gypsy music—either from desire or by SS orders. Roman Mirga recalled hearing the Gypsy violins playing as the "smouldering stench of roasting meat" from the belching chimneys came through the window. The music was being used "to calm the Jews going inside, soap and towels in their hands.... Except that it was not a bathhouse, but a crematorium. The Gypsy orchestra was there, my father was there, their music helping to make a smooth transition for the Jews from life to death."[24]

Mirga remembered another time when Dr. Mengele ordered Mirga's father awakened and introduced him to Commandant Höss. "This is the artist," Mengele said to Höss. "Play, Gypsy, play now for the Commandant—Brahms, Liszt, or Bartok."

> [H]is violin solos echoed across the camp, not only for the Nazis, but also for all the Gypsies, because he knew that they were listening—the Keldari king, Janusz Kwiek; the Gypsy noblemen, the Majewskis and the Sadowskis; the Polska Roma and Bergitka Roma, the Keldari, the Lowari, the Sinti. They were all listening and his music gave them strength to go on and to hope against hope that they would survive.[25]

Perhaps it was this small recollection of the past, this link to happier times, when the violins sang instead of wept, that helped some of the inmates retain their sanity.

THE OTHER INFAMOUS CAMPS

Although Auschwitz-Birkenau is probably the death camp most recognized by the public, Gypsies were also annihilated at many other installations. Hundreds were killed at Treblinka in the summer of 1942 and later in February of 1943. Some were brought to the camp in their wagons while others arrived in special railroad cars. "Small groups of Gypsies, a family or a few individuals who were brought to Treblinka, were shot at the Lazarett (hospital) rather than being taken to the gas chambers."[26] It is interesting to note that, unlike the Jews, the Gypsies' clothing and belongings were not sorted and retained, but were destroyed or thrown outside the camp and burned there. Apparently, what little the Gypsies possessed was so frayed and soiled that even the Nazis would not find use for it. Jacob Wiernik recalled that approximately 1,000 Gypsies were brought into the camp in the spring of 1943 in several transports; he described their possessions as "filthy rags, torn bedding, and other beggar's belongings.... All the Gypsies were taken to the gas chambers and then burned."[27]

The Lodz ghetto in Poland may have been the first locality to be utilized "in the initial extermination of Gypsies in a camp setting."[28] Reports vary because the Gypsy camp was closed off from outsiders except for a few physicians, hospital orderlies, and Jewish gravediggers, most of whom were later murdered. Rumors even circulated that the Gypsy prisoners

(*Zigeunerlager*) were, in fact, not Gypsies but members of the Balkans' intelligentsia destined for extermination. However, witnesses testified to seeing the arrival of transports carrying men, women, and children in typical Gypsy dress.[29]

For this one Gypsy camp, documents do exist showing that most of the Lodz Gypsies came from Austria and were predominantly Sinti, although members of the Kelderasz and Lowari clans were also represented. Meticulous lists were maintained of the possessions taken from the internees. A detailed accounting of items taken from Vienna Gypsies named Weinrich included gold watches, brooches and rings, diamond earrings, a chain approximately four feet in length with two gold pendants, and other items.[30]

Shortly after the Gypsies' arrival, a typhus epidemic occurred and many prisoners died. Surviving doctors, hospital workers, or gravediggers also testified to the brutality behind many deaths and to the inaccuracy in reporting the cause of death on death certificates. One worker in the Jewish cemetery stated that he had buried Gypsies, old people and young children, all of the corpses battered and some with marks indicating they had been hanged, rather than having died of natural causes. Later he found that Gypsies had been ordered to hang their own kin. Many of the bodies were hacked apart and had broken arms and legs. A doctor indicated that he had been forced to sign death certificates stating that the victims had died of a heart problem when, actually, the causes of death had been hanging or suffocation.[31]

From the Lodz ghetto, many Gypsies, along with Jews, were sent to the Chelmno extermination camp in March and April, 1942. Smaller transports of the Rom also went to other Jewish ghettos where they would suffer the same fate as the Jews. An escapee from Chelmno wrote a letter to his relatives which detailed the atrocities committed against the Gypsies there:

> The place where everyone is being put to death is called Chelmno.... People are killed in one of two ways: either by shooting or by poison gas.... Recently, thousands of Gypsies have been brought there from the so-called Gypsy camp in Lodz, and the same is done to them.[32]

Apparently at Chelmno, whole communities of Gypsies and Jews were being gassed continuously. Of the first Gypsies who had arrived from the Lodz ghetto, one source reports:

> All were gassed. With them was a Jewish doctor, Dr. Fickelburg, and a Jewish nurse, whose name is unknown. They had been working as a medical team in the Gypsy section of the [Lodz] ghetto. They too were gassed.[33]

There are mixed accounts on whether or not Gypsies were interned in Belzec and Sobibor. A Jewish survivor from Sobibor indicated that he remembered Gypsies arriving in the camp, and a Polish woman who lived in Belzec township gave testimony that she had seen Germans bringing Gypsies to Belzec in 1942. Although it was not determined whether the Gypsies were put to death, the woman indicated that "[t]he Gypsies implored on their knees to be released."[34]

In Germany itself, as early as 1938, 1,000 German Gypsy men and boys were sent to Buchenwald where they were joined in 1939 by 1,400 Austrian Gypsies transferred from Dachau. Since, as in Auschwitz, some Gypsies were not registered as such, and since individuals or families were sometimes committed without being registered, it is difficult to get an accurate number of those interned, released, or killed. Although thousands of Gypsies arrived at Buchenwald from widely scattered parts of Europe—Bohemia, Croatia, France, Carpathia, Ruthemia, Poland, Germany, and other camps such as Auschwitz, when the Gypsy camp there was abandoned—by late 1944 only a few remained in the camp, mainly from Germany.[35]

Part of the overflow from Auschwitz were kept only temporarily at Buchenwald and then sent on to another overflow or satellite camp called Dora. This overflow, about 1,800 in all, included Gypsies transferred from French camps as well as German Gypsies. In the autumn of 1944, many of the children were sent—on what would be a return journey for some—to Auschwitz for extermination. One source recalled:

> Even hardened prisoners were deeply moved when the SS in the fall of 1944 singled out and herded together all Jewish and Gypsy youngsters. The screaming, sobbing children, frantically trying to get to their fathers or protectors...were surrounded by a wall of carbines and machine pistols and taken away...for gassing.[36]

And, as at Auschwitz, someone had to bury the victims. A Jewish survivor from a team of eight gravediggers at Chelmno told of a "gas van" loaded with Gypsies which parked about 100 meters from where the eight men had dug a huge grave. The driver of the van would press a button and then get out of the van and move some distance away.

> At the same moment frightful screaming, shouting, and banging against the sides of the van could be heard. Then the driver reboarded the van and shone an electric torch into the back to see if the people were already dead. Then he drove the van to a distance of five metres from the ditch.[37]

Apparently, working with the dead bodies which had been heaped up "higgledy-piggledy...and were still warm and looked asleep" was a means of personal survival. However, if a man was not strong enough to continue the daily digging task, he was usually tossed into the mass grave and then shot by the SS guards. As weeks passed, the gruesome task must have become almost routine and a numbness would set in. Sometimes after the men had finished their labor, "they put on Gypsy clothes because of the cold and sat down on top of the corpses. It was a tragic-comic sight."[38]

For many Gypsies, the odyssey from one internment camp to another was continuous, as they were reshuffled across the Continent. Kurt Ansin was a good example of this, being sent first to Buchenwald, with his father, in 1938. From there he was moved to the Gypsy camp Am Holzweg in Magdeburg. In 1943, he was among those Gypsies who were anatomically measured by Dr. Ritter and Eva Justin for their studies into biological origins. From Am Holzweg Kurt was sent to Auschwitz, where he witnessed the shooting of his brother, who had spent five years in the German Army. Later, Kurt was again moved to Buchenwald, to the overflow camps Ellrich and Harzung, and finally took part in a forced march to Czechoslovakia.[39] Kurt was one of the few who survived.

Like Ansin, some Gypsies survived because they were able to continue laboring for the Nazis. However, even in the labor camps, death was always present. Katja H. recalled a sad incident from her family's days in the labor camp at Marburg. The men and women were in separate parts of the camp, as were the Gypsy children.

I remember my cousin was in the barracks with us children. She was a little older than I was. One day when the rest of us were out for roll call in front of the barracks, she didn't join us. She was so ill that she had stayed on her bunk. We knew she was suffering from typhus and too ill to do her usual work. When we went back inside, she was gone.

Shortly thereafter, word spread to my uncle that his daughter's body was lying on a heap of corpses. He ran to this huge pile of dead bodies and found her there; her arms and legs were twitching, so she was still alive. But the guards came and beat him about the head until they chased him away. She lay on that heap of bodies until she expired.

Of Katja's uncle, aunt, and six cousins, only the uncle would survive the rigors of internment. Yet those dead are remembered only by Katja and her uncle for they do not appear on any official death list.

Still, in most of these camps (as in Auschwitz) the Rom continued to eke out a daily existence. In Buchenwald (as in Auschwitz) there was a prisoner's band which had been formed in 1938, shortly after the camp was put into operation. Gypsies with their guitars and harmonicas "who produced a somewhat feeble brand of music" were eventually joined by trombone, drum, and trumpet players. Musical instruments had to be purchased by the band members, who worked in the carpenter shop or lumberyard by day and could rehearse only after hours. Eugen Kogon recounts hearing the Gypsy music one winter night and the feelings it evoked in him.

I remember New Year's Eve of 1939.... The night was clear, and even sorrow and terror seemed to have stiffened into frost.... Suddenly the sound of a Gypsy violin drifted out from one of the barracks... as though from happier times... tunes from the Hungarian steppe, melodies from Vienna and Budapest, songs from home.... It was ghastly to watch and hear the Gypsies... while exhausted prisoners carried their dead and dying comrades into camp.[40]

Although these tunes from the their former lives may have momentarily taken the Gypsies' thoughts back to happier times and helped ease their present suffering, their music could not help the Gypsies evade their future. No matter whether they died from the rigors of daily life in confinement or were exterminated by hanging, bullets, or gas, hundreds of thousands of Gypsies ceased to exist—some say up to one-third of all European

Gypsies were dead at the end of World War II.[41] Simon Wiesenthal estimates that over 1 million Gypsies "perished in extermination camps.... And the Nazis would have gassed six million if the Gypsies had been as numerous" as the Jews.[42] Miriam Novitch puts the figure even higher: "Between 70 and 80 percent of all Romani lives in Nazi-controlled territories have been destroyed, between one-half and three-quarters of the entire world population."[43] One-half to three-quarters of the entire number of Gypsies in the world—the figures are astounding!

When the stories of life in the Nazi concentration camps are told by Gypsies, it is difficult to comprehend how any survived the seemingly endless years of starvation, disease, torture, and murder. Of course, for a few of the Gypsy families, mobility and caution came to their rescue, and they evaded capture; for those confined to any of the 2,000 camps where there is evidence of Gypsy internees, the fact that they were allowed to maintain some semblance of close family life may have been their salvation. For too many others, gassing or the crematorium was to be their fate. Even before World War II had begun, these nonviolent people had been stereotyped as "asocial" and "racially unpure." It was only a matter of time until members of the Third Reich would find a means to solve their "Gypsy problem." Unfortunately, for many of the Gypsies, life in the decades after the war would bring little improvement.

Six

☙

Free At Last

*There surged around me an evil-smelling horde; men and boys reached out
to touch me. They were in rags and the remnants of uniforms. Death had
already marked many of them, but they were smiling with their eyes...
there was applause from the men too weak to get out of bed. It sounded like
the hand-clapping of babies.*
                                      —Edward R. Murrow, Buchenwald, April 15, 1945

𝒩EITHER THE WARM SPRING sunshine nor the newly budded trees could
erase the tension behind the barbed wire. Just as the news of the invasion
of Europe had earlier seeped into the camps, now in 1945 rumors of immi-
nent liberation began to reach those prisoners who had thus far escaped
Hitler's "final solution."

Also caught up in the rumors were the camp authorities who realized
that surrender could, at best, be delayed only a short time. As the allies
inched their way into Germany and Poland, the desperate German Army
conscripted men of every ethnic group from the prison camps to replace
fallen soldiers. This conscription took from among the starved and sick
those prisoners still fit enough to work or to carry arms. (It was at this time
that Pollo's father, Hans, was taken from Sachsenhausen and once again
found himself a member of the Wehrmacht.)

When it became ever more evident that defeat was inevitable, the SS
scurried to erase evidence of its atrocities. Records of internees were
burned hurriedly, prisoners were shuffled from camp to camp, and executions were intensified. But the evidence which would stun the world was
too massive to be concealed or destroyed.

Camps were liberated by the Allied forces beginning in the early part
of 1945. On April 15, 1945, British forces liberating Bergen-Belsen found
mostly Jews, but also several hundred Gypsies.[1] In the 1960s, while attempting through the German courts to get reparations from the German

government for her treatment in Bergen-Belsen, Sinti Sonja S. recalled the days at Bergen-Belsen shortly before liberation.

> We lived through an air raid at the camp. But they didn't throw bombs but leaflets. And in some of the containers that the planes dropped was some food.
>
> Quite a few of the inmates didn't know it was not a real air raid and against standing orders not to, they ran out of the barracks. The guards shot with machine guns. Terribly many people got killed that day. That way the SS remained masters of the situation.

On April 14, the day before Bergen-Belsen's liberation, large amounts of food were suddenly prepared by the guards and offered to the starving prisoners. Sonja remembered that they were offered huge pots of meat stew with carrots—food that they had not seen in years. The pots of stew were placed out in the middle of the parade ground for everyone to see and smell. The enticing odors emanating from the pots permeated the camp and drew some of the prisoners toward the food.

> As the first few people begin to approach them, they are getting shot by the guards. This may have been a trick not to arouse suspicion for if the food had been given too readily, people would have wondered and perhaps not eaten it for fear that it was tampered with.
>
> Eventually many could not resist the temptation to eat; the guards no longer shot at them and they ate. But my mother kept us from going to the pots even though we were starving and begged to do so. She said she had a funny feeling. She was right. The stew was poisoned. All who ate died of the poison.
>
> Up until the end the SS wanted to destroy all of us. Thousands died on this last day—Gypsies, Jews, who knew what some of them were. There was no one to care. The street into the camp was strewn with corpses. When the British arrived to liberate us, our SS tormentors were forced by the Tommies to clear the streets of the corpses.

Four days before the liberation of Bergen-Belsen, the American troops had marched into the horrors of Buchenwald. The liberators were totally shocked by what they encountered. In and around the compound were dead and wounded. Hordes of emaciated men, women, and children who had survived the final days stood on the parade ground or hobbled toward them. Those too ill or too fearful to emerge from the barracks huddled in their bunks or cowered in corners of the latrines. The stench from the dead and dying was overpowering. A British Army review reported:

> Evidence of cannibalism was found. The inmates had lost all self-respect, were degraded morally to the level of beasts. Their clothes were in rags, teeming with lice, and both inside and outside the huts was an almost continuous carpet of dead bodies, human excreta, rags and filth.[2]

Manfri Wood, a Gypsy member of a British Royal Air Force liberation team entering Bergen-Belsen, recalled that the men saw heaps of unburied bodies. In the camp the group found some Gypsy survivors.

> When I saw the surviving Romanies, with young children among them, I was shaken. Then I went over to the ovens, and found on one of the steel stretchers the half-charred body of a girl, and I understood in one awful minute what had been going on there.[3]

In all the camps, the same conditions were in evidence. At the first camp liberated by the Americans, Ohrdruf Nord near Gotha, one witness recalled that upon viewing the carnage in the slave labor camp General George S. Patton "was so moved physically that he vomited.... In one room where there were piled up twenty or thirty naked men, killed by starvation, Patton would not even enter. He said he would get sick if he did so."[4]

What greeted American Army generals Patton, Dwight D. Eisenhower, and Omar N. Bradley were some 3,000 corpses with lice crawling over them, "scabbed black where they had been gutted to provide a meal for the famished survivors."[5] Patton's chief of staff, Hobart Gay, wrote in his journal that the surviving inmates were all in such a bad state of starvation that even those who lived would never recover mentally. "No race," he wrote, "except a people dominated by an ideology of sadism could have committed such gruesome crimes...."[6]

In a letter to his wife, Beatrice, Patton attempted to describe what he had seen but simply could not find the words to do so.

> ...one of the most appalling sights I have ever seen.... Honestly, words are inadequate to express the horror of those institutions.[7]

General Eisenhower similarly had difficulty relating the impact Ohrdruf Nord had on him. Writing to his wife, Mamie, on April 15, 1945, the general mentioned that he had visited a German internment camp and that he "never dreamed that such cruelty, bestiality, and savagery could really exist in this world! It was horrible."[8]

Eisenhower also wrote to General George C. Marshall the same day, indicating that he had recently made a tour of the forward areas where he encountered "a most interesting, although horrible sight" at an internment camp near the town of Gotha.

> The things I saw beggar description.... The visual evidence and the verbal testimony of starvation, cruelty, and bestiality were so overpowering as to leave me a bit sick. In one room [there] were piled up twenty or thirty naked men, killed by starvation, George Patton would not even enter.[9]

On April 19, 1945, Eisenhower sent Cable FWD 19461 to General Marshall indicating more concentration camps were being found.

> We continue to uncover German concentration camps for political prisoners in which conditions of indescribable horror prevail. I have visited one of these myself and I assure you that whatever has been printed on them to date has been understatement. If you would see any advantage in asking about a dozen leaders of Congress and a dozen prominent editors to make a short visit to this theatre in a couple of C-54s, I will arrange to have them conducted to one of these places where the evidence of bestiality and cruelty is so overpowering as to leave no doubt in their minds about the normal practices of the Germans in these camps. I am hopeful that some British individuals in similar categories will visit the northern area to witness similar evidence of atrocity.[10]

Shortly thereafter, the general saw to it that both U.S. congressmen and British MPs visited the camps; in addition, he sent photographs to Prime Minister Churchill.[11]

Eisenhower had made the concentration camp visit deliberately and had taken great care to make a thorough inspection. He felt that if, in the future, allegations were made that what had happened in the concentration camps was merely "propaganda," he could testify and give firsthand information on the atrocities. The general had great foresight; this is exactly what is happening today.

Within a few weeks, most camps would be liberated and brought under the administration of the Americans, British, French, or Russians. However, not all prisoners were in camps at the time of liberation. Many were still being shuffled around the countryside under guard by remnants of the German Army. Pollo R., who had been interned in block 56 in the main camp in Buchenwald and in block III in Dora Sangerhausen (the satellite camp) was en route from Buchenwald to Ravensbrück. Suffering from pneumonia, he had been offered the chance to stay at the Buchenwald hospital and await the arrival of Red Cross personnel.

> I had a funny feeling. Everyone knew the hospital never really was a hospital. It was a prelude to death. It was the place you waited when you were too ill and feeble to work before they sent you on to the gas chambers or gave you the death shot [a lethal injection].

So, although he would have liked to stay in the camp, Pollo convinced the guards that he was well enough to go on the march to Ravensbrück and to keep up with the others. This was a lucky decision on his part, because the marchers were just out of sight of the camp when there was a gigantic explosion. The hospital had been blown up. "The reason I learned it was the hospital was that one of our SS guards mentioned it."

However, Pollo R. was in Ravensbrück barely three weeks before he was again on the move.

> In Ravensbrück I didn't work there. There was nothing much to do. It was only shortly before the curtain would fall. There was only escape, escape on the minds of the SS. They didn't know what to do with us, and we all were waiting that they would shoot us, as they were scared and desperate. The camps were being emptied because on one side came the Americans and the British closer and closer. And from the other side came the Russians.
>
> So we marched out of Ravensbrück and in the forest the guards suddenly shouted, 'Lie down! All lie face down, and don't anybody lift your head. He who will lift his head will be shot!' It came as no surprise. We thought we were done for as rumors had told us this was the way it would be done, all of us face down. Then we thought now that we made it this far, because we knew the Americans and the British would soon be coming, just to end like this, face down in the mud.

We must have lain there hour after hour in the dirt in the forest, too afraid to make a move, when we heard the humming of engines and heavy machinery. It was the tanks. I don't know what happened to the guards; they must have run further into the forest, but then we heard someone saying in Russian, "Get up! Get up!" The Russian soldiers had saved us. The joy, of course, was great!

When one reads Pollo R.'s comments, they seem an understatement. Yet today, forty years later, when he says quietly, "The joy, of course, was great," tears well up in his eyes and he is unable to continue.

Asked, "What was the first thing you did when you saw the Russians?" Pollo replied, "I wept! We now knew that we were free." However, he is quick to add that even a year later he was still looking over his shoulder to see if there were a person with a machine gun or a club standing behind him. Often today, he still awakens, *"der kalte Schweiss ist über mich"* [in a cold sweat] from nightmares of these times.

Each one of the survivors tells a different story about liberation, and yet each narrative is only a small variation on the same theme. In Bergen-Belsen, inmates heard the blare of a loudspeaker, "Hello, hello, you are free! We are British soldiers, and we came to liberate you!"[12] In camps all over Europe, hundreds of screaming, laughing, crying survivors crawled or hobbled toward their liberators.

BITTERSWEET FREEDOM

While the liberation created joy for the prisoners, it created enormous problems for the liberators. All of the camp inmates were malnourished; most were physically and emotionally ill and disabled from years of torture and abuse. Still, the liberators began the task of restoring broken bodies.

Pollo remembered that the Russian troops treated the prisoners very well. The group was taken to a "collection camp" where the ill were immediately tended to. Roman Ramati also documented his liberation by the Russians, who provided him with food and drink.[13] He indicates that he had been given permission to hide in a cellar on a Polish farm when Russian troops arrived.

One of them called, a boy in a Red Army uniform with just a hint of a moustache over his upper lip. "You are free!"... We embraced the two men. "The Germans have run away...."

Then several Russian soldiers entered the house, bringing with them vodka, sausages, and tins of sardines.... "Na zdarowie!" The Russian soldiers raised their glasses and we all drank. We downed not just one but at least three glasses.... "The war has ended for you," the corporal said.... We waved good-bye to them as their armored car pulled away across the field and then followed a side path that led to the road. That day was January 18, 1945, the day I was certain that, no matter how many Gypsies had died in camps or had been shot on the roads, the Gypsy nation had survived.[14]

Pollo R. was not detained long with the Russians. Because he had originally been interned from the western part of Germany, Pollo was returned with other released prisoners near that area. Eventually, he ended up with the American troops.

American G.I.'s, seeing camp victims' emaciated bodies and trying to help, were prone to distribute whatever rations they had in their gear. Instead of aiding the prisoners, often the food merely made the recipients extremely ill. Lieutenant Colonel Edward A. Zimmermann, M.D., head of an army unit sent into Dachau to aid those recently liberated, would later tell his family that, although the former prisoners badly needed nourishment, many individuals had to be placed in hospitals and fed intravenously for up to two months because their stomachs simply could not tolerate solid food.[15]

Pollo also discussed the problems he and other released prisoners had with trying to regain their strength.

> I was then 17 years old, and I weighed 38 kilograms [about 76 pounds]. I was very undernourished and was tended to by American soldiers. They gave me *Haferschleim* [a kind of smooth wheat cereal] because I could not eat. I had to be lifted up to eat. There were many others like me, wanting to eat but not able to do so.
>
> Then, we got CARE packages, but many people died because of these. They literally ate themselves to death. Their stomachs exploded from too much food too quickly. When the Americans saw that happening, they stopped giving the packages to us but kept them for us until we could handle solid food again.

The most pressing need for the freed prisoners was medical aid. Camps were rife with dysentery, typhus, and tuberculosis. Many of the liberated would only have a few hours or a few days of freedom before they died. Throughout most camps, despite medical aid and food rushed in by the Allies, in the first week of freedom several hundred a day died. In the following weeks death rates were still being reported at several hundred a week.

For Erika S., the little sister of Sonja S., freedom came too late. Erika had starved to death. Although Sonja had taken on one of the more horrible jobs disposing of corpses in order to get extra bread rations for Erika, it had not been enough. Days before liberation Erika had fallen into a state of apathy, no longer speaking or crying; she died within hours of being set free.

Of course, in all camps immediate medical attention was forthcoming, but to try and cope with the enormous number of appallingly abused released prisoners was a staggering undertaking. The British flew into Bergen-Belsen ninety-eight medical students along with nurses and doctors.[16] The Americans also established hospitals and provided desperately needed medical supplies. In one hospital Karl Stojka "underwent several operations for injuries sustained during beatings by Nazi concentration camp guards."[17] Pollo R. was in an American Army hospital for three weeks where they "fattened me up so that I looked more like a human being instead of a skeleton." Then, because there was a shortage of medical facilities in Germany, he was one of the many juveniles who were shipped to hospitals in Switzerland.

> The Americans determined that we go to Switzerland. They wanted that we have the best medical treatment available, because in Germany there was nothing, neither food nor medicine. And what was there was what the Americans had brought, but they didn't have that much because they were not prepared for something like this [the number of holocaust survivors]. In Switzerland there was everything available.

Pollo was hospitalized in Bern, Switzerland, for over six months for treatment of tuberculosis, which he had contracted from the deplorable conditions in Auschwitz and on the forced "death marches" between the various camps. Although he was now comfortably located in the hospital recuperating, warm and well-fed, "his heart was restless." Constantly, he wondered what fate had befallen the rest of his family since his separation from them. He waited impatiently for the time when he would be free of his illness and allowed to return to Germany and begin the job of locating any survivors.

LIFE AFTER LIBERATION

At the end of World War II, the liberated countries of Europe were awash with a flood of displaced persons (DPs) attempting to relocate from one Occupied zone to another, to emigrate to other countries, or to find missing loved ones and rebuild their former lives. However, survival would continue to be a struggle. Entire sections of cities had been demolished by bombs and shells. The armies crisscrossing the countryside had played havoc with farming, and food was extremely scarce. To complicate matters, the winter of 1946 was one of the coldest in European history.

While a few Gypsies were physically well enough to leave the camps and return to their former homes, they often found many of their family members missing or dead and learned that they were the last of their clans. Another problem Gypsies encountered in some regions of Germany was an old law which stated that those coming out of concentration camps without any form of employment could be arrested and sent to labor camps.[18] Thus, before many could find gainful employment or return to their prewar style of living, they merely exchanged life in one camp for life in another camp or holding area.

Like other displaced persons in Europe, the Gypsies wandered the countryside, spending the nights in the open or, if lucky, in a barn some farmer was willing to let them use. Others found temporary shelter among the ruins of buildings in Europe's ravaged cities. One American G.I. recalled seeing several Gypsy families on the roads with other refugees. "You could tell the Gypsies from the others because they were very dark skinned and kept to themselves...apart from the other stragglers...their own family group. We talked with some of them and gave them food since they had none. No one seemed to care what happened to them."

The surviving members of Pollo R.'s family made their way out of Bergen-Belsen in the back of a British truck toward the home they had left in 1940. Although they were fearful that everything would have changed greatly, they were happy to find their house relatively intact. Still, "they were laughing with one eye and crying out of the other," for the ghosts of the past were in Krefeld. Since they had last been in the city, many siblings had died; aunts, uncles, and cousins had also perished in the camps; the fate of friends was unknown. The last time the family had seen Pollo was when he was transported from Auschwitz-Birkenau, and they assumed that he was dead.

Although Pollo's home had been occupied by the family of an SS officer during the war, the German family had been moved out by the British when they occupied Krefeld. To their delight, Pollo's family discovered that, compared to many, their house was in fairly good shape and its few remaining furnishings were usable. Like the rest of the Gypsy population, the family gradually began to pick up the pieces of their lives.

Pollo R. returned to Krefeld for Christmas of 1945 and was reunited with his family—sadly, a considerably smaller family. By then, his mother, who had never fully recovered from her years in the camps, lay dying. Of his sixteen brothers and sisters who were originally interned in 1940, only three sisters and two brothers remained alive. Months later, Hans would return, and Pollo would hear the story of his father's survival.

After Hans R. had been taken from camp and reinstated in the Wehrmacht, he was sent to the crumbling Eastern front. Captured with other Germans by Russian soldiers, he was scheduled to be shot. Ironically, his tattoo from Auschwitz was seen by a Russian, and he was spared the fate of the other Germans. Still, he would be held in Flensburg with other prisoners of war for nearly eighteen months after the liberation of the concentration camps before being reunited with his family.

On the way back to Munich, Katja H. and her surviving family were fortunate enough to ride a few miles on a farmer's cart. However, most of the long journey from the labor camp where they had been interned was made on foot. The family moved in with an aunt who lived approximately twenty kilometers outside of Munich. The aunt, because she had been married to a German soldier, had not been arrested and interned with other Gypsies in her neighborhood. She permitted the entire group to stay in her tiny apartment, although it was extremely crowded. As Sonja said, "We had a spot, maybe one bedroom and half of a kitchen, and we were fourteen people there. We slept on the floor, but to us it was heaven."

According to Katja, finding food took up a major portion of every day, for both the camp survivors and the general population.

For food, you hunted in the fields; you dug; you stole a chicken or a loaf of bread if you could find it. The black market was very active if you had money. If you didn't, you went hungry. Although it [the black market] became even more active when the Americans came and brought all kinds of things people needed and hadn't seen for a very long time. We were always hungry, never satisfied, in the day or at night. The whole day was spent just trying to get enough together to survive until the next morning.

And the Germans did the same thing as we did as they had nothing, too. The Germans stole from each other. They broke into cellars what was bombed, looking for canned food or something that could be marketed for food. The Germans were in the same spot we were in.

Katja H. remembered that, later, things became somewhat easier when the Americans arrived, established a semblance of order, and allotted rations to the starving population. "We got first choice. For the concentration camp people, you showed the authorities that you had been in the camps." Upon presenting evidence of her internment, Katja received a stamped document, indicating she had been a prisoner. "It was a credential showing you were like a prisoner of war—you were a prisoner of the German state."

Although the Allies did their best to quickly resettle the displaced persons, the overwhelming number made this impossible. For many there was an indeterminate period in displaced persons' camps. Because accommodations were so scarce, oftentimes the former prisoners had to share quarters with former SS men and other pro-Nazis. "Remnants of the families who had been put behind barbed wire at the Düsseldorf-Lierenfeld holding camp before the war found themselves in the same barracks when they returned [supposedly liberated]."[19]

Some of the single survivors and orphaned children ran afoul of the military Occupation authorities as well as the new German civil law. If the displaced persons' cards were lost, if records in the UN relief agency were misplaced, if they had served a prison sentence prior to the war, a deportation order could be issued or they would simply be told to leave Germany. Since many Gypsies were unable to obtain admission to other countries, they were reimprisoned and served additional time in camps. Emotionally distraught from their harsh treatment at the hands of the Nazis, concentration camp survivors, seeking revenge or justice, occasionally preyed upon those Germans who had not been imprisoned, and they sometimes assaulted and murdered known Nazis. "The military courts, determined to make stern examples to reestablish order and authority, passed the death sentence and long prison terms on numbers of people, including Gypsies...."[20]

One may wonder why, like many other displaced persons, the Gypsies did not leave Europe. Surviving Jews and other war-weary individuals fled in droves to Israel, the United States, South America, Canada, Australia. The Gypsies, however, had no country of their own, no relatives to sponsor them in a new nation, no knowledge of the intricacies of emigration. Their people had been a part of the European population for 1,000 years. They would continue to be so. Almost all merely returned to the areas from which they had originally been rounded up and began the job of rebuilding their lives.

Little by little, like the rest of the European population, the Gypsies' existence returned to some semblance of normality. Many of the Rom again took up their nomadic lifestyles, wandering in the latter part of the 1940s and early 1950s through the devastated towns and countryside. The Sinti found their way back into the cities to jobs or businesses they had held or owned before the war. But the horrors of the camps were always with them—in their memories, in their dreams. As the wife of one man told the authors, "You talk with him now; he is OK. But he was an 'old man' when he got out of the camps. He was young, but his body was old. His mind was old. Tonight he will have the nightmares of old. The old fears are still there."

Perhaps this one word—fear—best describes the holocaust. Wanda G. says the unbelievable fear she experienced when she was a part of the experiments on Gypsy children is always with her. "I can sometimes almost see the hospital rooms, the medical tools. I can't believe it is all over. I seem to still feel the pain, somewhere inside me—maybe only in my mind." Sonja S. says she has a fear that she will again have to experience the extreme pangs of hunger and the bitter cold as she did in Birkenau. Pollo says the fear is always lurking in his mind that the "camps can come again." With the rise of the neo-Nazi movement, with resumption of Gypsy persecution in these past four decades, and with the open deportation of Gypsies throughout Europe, perhaps all have a reason to fear.

Seven

The "Gypsy Problem" Continues

The only weapon with which I can defeat is a flame-thrower;
I will exterminate all Gypsies; adults and children;
Although they can only be destroyed if we cooperate.
If we exterminate them successfully
We shall have a land free of Gypsies.

PROPAGANDA LYRICS FROM HITLER'S Third Reich? No. These are lyrics from a popular song by a Hungarian group called Mosoly at the Mosaic Club in Budapest in 1987.[1] According to a 1990 survey, racial prejudice is growing in Hungary. The survey revealed that almost "three-quarters of the population were hostile to Romani people."[2] The "Gypsy problem" persists as a major issue in all of Europe.

In Germany, blamed by many for the nation's economic ills, Roma have become scapegoats for the antiforeigner movement and are frequent targets for neo-Nazi and skinhead violence. During August 1992, this anti-Roma hatred culminated when a refugee hostel in Rostock, housing 200 Rumanian Gypsies, was firebombed by an estimated 1,000 German youths. Gypsies have been fleeing Rumania since the 1989 revolution, attempting to escape mob violence and pogroms[3]—violence which the Rumanian government appears to support.

The history of the 1930s is being repeated; yet much of the world is oblivious to the plight of the Rom. Throughout Europe (and even in the United States) persecution of and discrimination against Gypsies is tolerated, and in many instances, encouraged. Is it any wonder, then, that many Gypsies continue to live in a climate of anxiety and fear?

"They [the German government] threatened to fine me 10,000 marks (roughly 4,000 American dollars)," Pollo R. began, "for not registering for the census in 1988. But I wouldn't give them any information. I told them,

'You think I'm crazy? My father registered us in 1938 and look what happened to us—Auschwitz! You think I'm crazy enough to do this again? I said I would pay the fine.'" Pollo was silent for several minutes as he got his thoughts together.

> You know these are not good times. Be glad you are in America. The way things are right now, all they [the German people] need is a little Hitler. Then, they'll all be lifting their right arms and screaming "Heil" again.
>
> You know why I say that? Just last summer I was walking in a department store in Cologne, and I had on a shirt with short sleeves. Near me were two young Germans, and one noticed my number from Auschwitz on my arm. And what do you think he said? "Look at that guy over there. They forgot to gas him in Auschwitz." Maybe you understand now why I'm worried for my wife and children who are all in Germany.

Similar to the comments Pollo R. made, Katja H. indicated that she was glad to be in America where she felt that her Gypsy heritage would cause her fewer problems.

> Here I do not call attention to myself. By that I mean people cannot so easily look at my face and see a label "Gypsy." Here I can be any number of races—Greek, Indian, Italian, Mexican. That way I don't worry so much about my children having the fingers pointed at them. If at school, something should be missing, I don't want it said that "the Gypsies took it."

In Germany, the fear of being singled out as Gypsy rather than Aryan is constantly mentioned. "Particularly by the women," Katja continued. "You know they are looking at you. It's almost as if the rest of the population [German] could look at a lineup and say, 'OK. Gypsy, Aryan, Aryan, Aryan, Gypsy.'"

Interviews with other European Gypsies emphasize the same theme. One Gypsy woman married to an Aryan man recalled the birth of their first child. Unable to focus clearly, as her glasses had been removed during labor, she saw covering her child's skin the blood from the birth and in anguish thought, "Oh, my God! He came after my side of the family. His skin is dark. Now, everyone will know he is a Gypsy." After the baby was bathed, his mother was quite relieved to see that he appeared to be of a lighter complexion—"more Aryan."

Another German woman, an Aryan married for thirty years to a Gypsy, indicated in an interview that no one in the neighborhood where the couple lived knew that he had Gypsy blood. "He doesn't look like most Gypsies do," she emphasized. "His complexion is not too dark. We're lucky he was sterilized as a boy for we have no children. Otherwise, one child might have been dark skinned; then people would have known of his blood and none of us would have been accepted."

If there had been children and it was known that the children were part Gypsy, the woman explained, "they would be made the scapegoats at school and at play." Also, her husband's position at work would be in jeopardy if anyone thought he was of Gypsy origin. "But no one knows. Actually, we are fortunate; we fit in."[4]

In Vienna, a Gypsy named Charlie said that all Gypsies were fearful of what might again happen to them. As he rolled up his sleeve and pointed to a tattoo on his arm, he stated, "You want to know my real name? That's who I am—Z5742." Charlie had been sent to Auschwitz, Buchenwald, and Flossenburg and had witnessed his father's hanging and the murder of his mother, two sisters, and a brother. He was still afraid of those he called Nazis and of those who might perpetuate their doctrine.

Commenting on the allegations that President Kurt Waldheim of Austria had been involved in concentration camp slayings, Charlie stated:

> It is not Waldheim. We don't know who this Waldheim is, or what he did. But the people who wanted him to be president, these people don't like us. All the Gypsies are scared.[5]

Like Charlie, many other Gypsies also express the belief that it would be easy for Europe (and especially Germany) again to take up the genocidal behavior of the Nazis.

Part of their fear stems from the belief that no one cares about their past or future problems. They emphasize that, in the aftermath of World War II, while the world expressed outrage at the treatment of the Jews, the Gypsies were a forgotten minority. Many feel the war crimes trials did little to make people aware of their suffering and death at the hands of the Nazis and Nazi supporters.

NÜRNBERG AND AFTER

In the prosecutor's opening statement before the Nürnberg Military Tribunals, Gypsies *are* mentioned among the groups designated to be destroyed by Hitler's Einsatzgruppen. The defendants *were* charged with deliberate and systematic genocide, particularly in regard to Jews, Poles, and Gypsies. However, according to Ian Hancock (Gypsy name Yanko le Redzosko), secretary of the Romany Union, "Not one Gypsy was called to testify" at these trials.[6] Hancock also states that although West Germany paid nearly $715 million as restitution for the "war crimes" to Israel and various Jewish organizations, Gypsies as a group received nothing. In *The Destiny of Europe's Gypsies*, Gratton and Puxon also emphasize that the Gypsies received no restitution from the German government.

Most of what little information is available from the Nürnberg trials comes from answers German defendants provided during questioning; however, one has the feeling that, while their fate was occasionally mentioned during the trials, Gypsies were considered so unimportant in the hierarchy of victims that they existed and died almost as invisible people. For example: Asked at his trial about the number of Gypsies killed by troops under his command, defendant Otto Ohlendorff replied that he had no idea how many Gypsies his Kommandos had killed and denied that he had seen children killed. When questioned further about Gypsies, he seemed unable to separate Jews and Gypsies.

Q. On what basis did you kill Gypsies, just because they were Gypsies? Why were they a threat to the security of the Wehrmacht?

A. It is the same as for the Jews.

Q. Blood?

A. I think I can add up from my own knowledge of European history that the Jews actually during wars regularly carried on espionage service on both sides.

Judge. You were asked about Gypsies.

Q. I was asking you about Gypsies, as the Court points out, and not Jews. I would like to ask you now on what basis you determined that every Gypsy found in Russia should be executed, because of the danger to the German Wehrmacht?

A. There was no difference between Gypsies and Jews. At the time the same order existed for the Jews.[7]

Again the presiding judge reminded Ohlendorff that the court was trying to find out what he knew about Gypsies, not Jews, and asked if Gypsies had also participated in "political strategy and campaigns?"

Q. Is it also European history that Gypsies always participated in political strategy and campaigns?

A. Espionage organizations during campaigns.

Q. The Gypsies did?

A. The Gypsies in particular. I want to draw your recollection to extensive descriptions of the Thirty Years' War by Ricarda and Schiller—[8]

The judge interrupted and ended this line of questioning by indicating that Ohlendorff was going back extremely far for justification (the early 1600s). Throughout his testimony Ohlendorf consistently evaded the questions about Gypsy deaths or answered the questions by explaining why Jews were killed.

In addition to testimony by defendants, the military tribunal also cited official reports prepared by Einsatzgruppen and Einsatzkommando [Kommando] leaders. Intermingled with the reports of Jewish massacres are also an occasional mention of Gypsy deaths:

In the Crimea 1,000 Jews and Gypsies were executed. (No-2662)

In Simferopol [Russia], apart from Jews also the Krimchak and Gypsy question was solved. (No-3258)

...Now is the time to clean up with the war criminals, once and forever, to create for our descendants a more beautiful and eternal German. We don't sleep here. Every week 3-4 actions, one time gypsies, the other time Jews, partisan and other rabble.... (No-5655)[9]

The Simferopol operation is especially shocking in that the chief of Kommando group 11 b, who had been notified that he was expected to kill several thousand Jews and Gypsies before Christmas 1941, was not upset by the order. His main concern was that he would not have sufficient personnel, trucks, guns, and ammunition to adequately perform his mission. The mission was accomplished. "The Jews and Gypsies—men, women, and children—were in their graves by Christmas."[10]

It should be noted that the German defendants' ways of justifying their actions or avoiding any discussion of Gypsy victims in Europe's concentration camps became "the norm" for the rest of the European population. It also seemed to be the norm for the rest of the world. No one recorded survivors' testimonies of individual or group torture and death. No one questioned what happened to Gypsy families and Gypsy property. While most victims of the concentration camps were being rehabilitated, relocated, and paid reparations, the Gypsies were left to fend for themselves. They were simply forgotten.

THE "GYPSY PROBLEM" CONTINUES

The fact that Gypsies *had* been victims of the holocaust did not endear them to the postwar population of Europe as was the case with some other groups. "Contrary to the Jews, they were not considered victims of racial persecutions but only a special variety of 'asocials,' that the Third Reich had interned in concentration camps instead of rehabilitation centers."[11] Therefore, repressive measures against the Rom which had been in effect earlier in some countries would continue into the following decades, and new repressive measures would be initiated throughout all of Europe.

Once again, the question of who was or was not a "true" Gypsy would be debated in European nations. It began in England in the mid-1950s and reminded many of the debate in Germany in the 1930s. There had been a rash of tent or caravan dwellers roaming the English countryside after the war, and several parishes were attempting to legally evict these wanderers. The issue took on racial overtones as the debaters tried to set a distinction between the full-blooded Romany and those who had intermarried with other groups (sometimes referred to as travelers, Didecais, mumpers, jenische). While there was some sympathy in local communities for the "true" Gypsies, this was not the case for the half-breeds, as a report of the Hampshire Association of Parish Councils stated in 1960:

The old Romany stock is diluted and there has been an infiltration of "poor white." The majority of these people have wandered all their life. Though in the past, they had their proud traditions, they, and we too, as thinking people, are faced with the problem that besets a decadent stock. They belong to neither past nor present.[12]

A member of the English parliament went so far as to state that nothing can be done with *some* Gypsies and that "you must exterminate the impossibles." In England, Gypsies are confined to government reservations. The city of Bradford, for example, attempted to get a court injunction making it illegal "for Gypsies to trespass within the city limits."[13]

It is true that the government's Caravan Site Act of 1968 forced local English authorities to provide camping places for Gypsies, but many of the camps were located on rubble-strewn wasteground. As one Gypsy man commented, "They usually allocate wasteground on industrial estates or in decaying urban neighborhoods, or next to railway lines, highway overpasses, sewage treatment plants, and landfills."[14] Even these undesirable locations are not always guaranteed, as local citizens continue today to protest against having Gypsies in their home areas.

Perhaps one of the saddest commentaries on discrimination against Gypsies was shown in a 1987 letter from the Spanish and Portuguese Jews' Congregation in London to the Essex County Council protesting a planned Gypsy site on land opposite a cemetery, as the congregation feared the Gypsy trespassers would disturb the haven of rest. A stinging letter from Ian Hancock, expressing his shock that "a Jewish organization should lend its voice to anti-Gypsyism" had little effect on the other organization.[15]

Signs, leaflets, and cartoons also are utilized to constantly disparage the Gypsy population in England. "Please make sure that the car park is locked after use. Gypsies in the area," reads a sign in the London Borough of Islington. Leaflets circulated by the Conservative Campaign HQ state:

<u>GYPSIES</u>

FILTH; CRIME
ONE DAY AFTER THE
ELECTION WE
PROMISE TO MOVE
THEM OUT

Cartoons repeatedly show Gypsies being refused service in campsites, markets, or village pubs.

The Romani-Jewish Alliance Newsletter cites items in May and August 1993, from a Birmingham newspaper, *The Evening Mail*, which called Gypsies "the scum of the earth...parasites...and unwashed hordes" and set up a hotline to "help chase this scum out of the Midlands."[16] A recent study, "The Gypsy and the State," by Derek Hawes and Barbara Perez claims that policies toward Gypsies in Britain's Criminal Justice Act of 1994 amount to "ethnic cleansing" of the Rom who are seen as "an enormous threat."[17]

Of course, England should not be singled out as the chief example for Gypsy persecution in Europe. On the Continent "old ways" of discriminating against Gypsies are continually cropping up and persecution is ongoing and widespread. In Poland, where persecution should particularly be remembered, bigotry and intolerance seem to merely recreate the bitter scenes from the 1930s and 1940s.

Since 1981, there have been numerous reports of attacks on Gypsy settlements throughout Poland. The first attack occurred in the city of Konin, where enraged peasants overturned and burned Gypsy cars and wagons, wounding many Gypsy men, women, and children. The police reaction to all of this mayhem was to ignore the perpetrators, round up the Gypsies, and escort them out of town. Their advice was, "Go to another country where you will be better tolerated."[18]

Conditions are no better in other European nations. Whether they broke the law or not, a threatening 1985 edict in France gave police powers to "*deal* with all Gypsies" as they saw fit.[19] It was hoped that this law would encourage many Gypsies to leave France and would discourage others from entering the country.

Michel Sapin, the assistant to the mayor in the Paris suburb of Nanterre announced plans in early 1993 to "transfer" several hundred Gypsies from his suburb to a camp near Lyon, France. However, the residents of Lyon were not about to have Gypsies in their area. When they blocked access roads and threatened to bring guns to keep the "invasion" of Gypsies out, the prime minister announced that plans to move the Rom had been scrapped.[20]

In the former Yugoslavia, according to the Anti-Slavery Society (London), Gypsy children are bought for $100 each and smuggled across the hills into Italy. An article entitled "Child Slave Trade in Yugoslavia" condemned this practice, in the May 1986 issue of the new Croatian home magazine *Hrvatska Domovina*. Some of these children had been trained as thieves, prostitutes, or intentionally mutilated so that they would be more effective as beggars.[21]

Prejudice and discrimination against Gypsies in Czechoslovakia permeates all facets of their lives, including housing, education, jobs, and recreation, even though a January 9, 1991, article of the Charter of Fundamental Rights and Freedoms expressly forbids this. Gypsies are forced to live in the less desirable sections of cities, are denied access to many forms of employment, and are often barred from restaurants, bars, and sports arenas. "Young Romany people have nowhere to play sports," states Anton Pusha from Puste. "The non-Romanies don't let us play in the same fields."[22]

Much more damaging, however, is the idea of "ethnic cleansing" which can still be found in the Czech culture. A late 1980s report from Josef Prokop, an official on the Czechoslovakian Commission for Problems of the Gypsy Populace, asserted that "those [Gypsies] who still maintained the traditional itinerant lifestyle were genetically unfit.... [W]e will also in the future pursue regulation of the birthrate of the unhealthy population."[23] One magazine did indicate that this government-sponsored program, which is attempting to prevent the birth of Romany children, to resettle various Gypsy communities, and to break down their strong cultural ties, sounded "like a leftover from the Third Reich."[24] Even with such adverse publicity in some publications and despite protests from various humanitarian organizations in the 1980s, a 1990 press release contends that in Czechoslovakia the "forced sterilization of Gypsy women and the permanent removal of their children for placement in government homes continues."[25]

Human Rights Watch reports that all during the Communist regime and as late as 1992, sterilization of Romany women was commonplace. Incentives such as money or furniture were given to women who would voluntarily consent to the operation, although the end result of the surgery was not always fully understood by the uneducated Gypsy females. Other Gypsy women were unknowingly sterilized after Caesarean births. K. F., an eighteen-year-old with two children, told how she learned she had been sterilized:

> I had just given birth, and I was unconscious after a Caesarean section. I had no idea I had been sterilized. A few weeks later I met my doctor on the street and he asked me, "Did I do a good job?" I said, "What do you mean?" He said, "So that you can't have children." That's how I found out. Nobody told me in the hospital.[26]

Excuses for the sterilizations of the Romany by non-Romanies range from control of "the growth of an unhealthy population" to the nebulous category "social reasons." Jiri Biolek, a pediatrician in an area of Northern Bohemia which is heavily populated by Gypsies, explained:

> No official politics for sterilization existed. I'm convinced that sometimes there was sterilization after a Caesarean section, when a very socially weak Romany woman, after having had six children, was sterilized without her knowledge. In my opinion, the gynecologist could find reasons for sterilizing a woman without her consent—for health reasons.... I think that the gynecologist had the right to do this without her consent. On the one hand, there are human rights. But on the other hand, when you see how these Gypsies multiply and you see that it is a population of an inferior quality, and when you look at the huge sums that had to be paid for the care of these children, it's understandable.[27]

Obviously, Dr. Biolek's rationalization for the concept of enforced sterilization of "inferior" or unwanted people is much the same as that used by the Third Reich and still suggested for various ethnic and racial groups in many countries around the world today.

In Hungary, police routinely permit the photographing of Gypsy juvenile suspects but not Hungarian juveniles. Punk groups call for a "Gypsy-free zone," and building walls sport graffiti such as "KTG"—Kill the Gypsy. Local leaders of various organizations blatantly state that the "new Hungarians" (the Gypsies) "should be locked up behind barbed wire."[28] Déjà vu of 1930s Germany?

Authorities in Romania consider all Gypsies "Romanians" (on a lower social and cultural level, of course) and insist they be integrated into the dominant society. While the Gypsies may use their Romany names at home, the authorities recognize only Romanian names; Romanian instead of the Romany language must be used publicly. Gypsies are not permitted to form societies which would help preserve their traditions and identity.[29] Integration here translates into obliteration of Gypsy culture.

Like the rest of Europe, the Belgians have their "Gypsy problem." Brussels, which lays claim to the title "the heart of Europe," forces Gypsies to carry at all times identification papers which are stamped "undetermined nationalities." Many of these so-called "stateless" Gypsies have roots in Belgium dating back several centuries. However, since 1975, there has been a law that requires Gypsies to register each year and request permission to continue residence, even though they were born in the country.

The Gypsies who live in caravans fare even worse. Not only do they have to get permission to camp, but local Belgians limit their stay at campsites from six to twenty-four hours. Usually police arrive with a tow truck and force the Gypsies back on the roads. When they stop at the next site, the scenario is repeated.[30] Obviously, this harassment eliminates any feelings of security or stability for the Gypsy family. It also contributes to the continuing illiteracy of the Gypsies since children are unable to attain an of education.

On the Iberian Peninsula, some very repressive laws are also still in effect. Since most of the Gypsies are not considered legal residents, Spain prohibits them from legally marrying; they have no right to vote nor do they have a right to social welfare. In the real sense they are outside the law and are denied a "normal" life in Spain. Many of them live in squalor on the outskirts of cities and villages, are in very poor health, and have an extremely high incidence of infant mortality. Most are considered to be habitual thieves.[31]

Although the Gypsies are nominally Catholic, Italy, the home of Catholicism, like other countries shows signs of prejudice and discrimination. An American businessman in Rome in the Spring of 1995 was astonished upon leaving Mass at Saint Peter's Cathedral to read a sign in an adjacent McDonald's restaurant warning customers to "Beware of Thieving Gypsies." During this same time frame American television and printed news told of several Gypsy boys being shot in Italy.

In Austria, where Sinti and Roma Gypsies have lived for over 300 years, violence continues. On February 4, 1995, a pipe bomb, hidden in a gravestone-shaped placard which read "Gypsies go back to India," exploded, killing four Gypsy men. The next day another bomb exploded in a nearby community. Responsibility for these bombings and others has been claimed by a neo-Nazi group calling itself the Bavarian Liberation Army.[32]

Ironically, even with its history of Gypsy genocide, Germany is still the country where many Gypsies seek to live. After World War II, West Germany desperately needed unskilled labor to help it rebuild. Thousands of Roma (nearly 30,000 according to one estimate) fleeing from Eastern Europe in hopes of finding a better life settled in shacks surrounding many of the larger German cities. Here they found themselves in trouble not only with the ethnic Germans but also with their brother Gypsies—the Sinti. The German Sinti, who were more integrated into the culture, often showed open hostility towards the recent arrivals, the Roma. Romani Rose, president of the German Sinti and Roma Organization, stated, "This is part of the Gypsy misfortune.... The behavior of some Gypsies towards others can be worse than that of non-Gypsies towards our race as a whole."[33]

Usually economically better off than the Roma (who often live in tents and slums, without steady employment), the German Sinti are themselves still subjected to prejudice and discrimination. Judges are accused of punishing Gypsies more harshly than non-Gypsies. Gypsy school children are often berated and beaten. One Gypsy wife commented upon a sign she had seen in Mannheim admonishing people to deposit rubbish in specific containers and not to "behave like Gypsies."[34] To the ethnic Germans, little distinction is made between Roma and the Sinti; both are simply *Zigeuner*.

For the traveling Roma, death sometimes awaits. In 1973, in Pfaffenhofen, Bavaria, two Gypsy women were shot and a third wounded by a farmer. Apparently, they had entered his farm in order to purchase fruits and vegetables. Interestingly, the farmer went free.[35]

For most Gypsies, however, there are simply the "everyday problems" to be encountered on the road. If they stop their caravans in a public parking place to cook something and feed the children, the police chase them away since they are prohibited from entering official camping sites. However, no alternative sites are provided. Yet some Gypsies feel they are better off in Germany than in other European countries, since the Germans have begun compensating the Sinti for the harsh World War II treatment by waiving taxes on any kind of business for them. Organized Gypsy movements in Germany also continue to demand equal rights for their people and the abolition of "special files" kept on Gypsies by the German police.[36] Just when these small gains are made in one area, deportation of Gypsies begins in another.

In late 1989, West Germany extended a much-publicized welcome to East German refugees fleeing from Communism. However, while the welcome mat was out for some refugees, others were not so fortunate. The West German states of North Rhine-Westphalia and Hamburg were attempting to expel thousands of Gypsies who had recently slipped in from Yugoslavia and Poland. Fifteen hundred Gypsies were selected for deportation in Hamburg. In Cologne, city officials proposed that the Roma be kept in an internment camp located on the site of a toxic waste dump. When questioned about this discriminatory treatment, some officials explained that Germans [from Eastern bloc countries] were freely admitted to West Germany because they were *ethnic* Germans. The Gypsies, on the other hand, were economic refugees, not political refugees, and wouldn't be persecuted if forced to return to Poland and Yugoslavia. German Chancellor Helmut Kohl "passed the buck" by stating that "the treatment of the Gypsies was the business of the individual German states."[37]

Gypsies attempted to fight back. A protest sit-in was staged in Hamburg at the Neuergamme Memorial—site of a former Nazi concentration camp. The Gypsies set up a camp at the memorial on August 29, 1989, attracting from 100 to 500 supporters from a nearby Gypsy community of 15,000 in Hamburg. Prompting the occupation of the camp was a dispute over the threatened expulsion of several Gypsy families and a proposal by the city of Hamburg for criteria which would allow Gypsies to remain—residence of at least four years, no criminal record, and at least partial integration into the German culture. "Why can't we stay?" Rudko Kawcaynski, the head of a Gypsy social welfare organization called the Roma and Sinti Union, was quoted as asking police who were sent to end the protest; "They [Germany] take in tens of thousands of resettlers and settlers from abroad. We're just a handful of people."[38]

A September 12, 1989, press release by SA-ROMA (Minneapolis) charged that "food, shelter, and sanitation facilities on the site are meager in part due to the refusal by German aid organizations, such as the German Red Cross, to give support. As of September 2, there were only two toilets and no provision for waste disposal in the entire camp." SA-ROMA also questioned why the Gypsies were being deported from Germany and felt that there was "no answer that does not smack of additional racial discrimination; an odd irony at this time of the widely publicized largesse in accepting East German refugees."[39]

The protest ended without violence and, perhaps, with some little degree of success. There was considerable publicity about the incident, and around the world Gypsy organizations protested West Germany's treatment of the Gypsies. Then, in December 1989, the Hamburg senate granted "renewable residency permits" to Gypsies.[40]

Other positive measures have also been enacted in several other European countries. In Holland, for example, a law states that although the nomads must get permission to live in a trailer, the local governments must provide them with the amenities of life such as water and electricity. Special education schools and kindergartens have been opened for the Gypsies and, besides the welfare payments which they receive, they are now eligible for housing loans.[41] The Church, municipal authorities, and social workers extend legal and other aid to anyone who gets into trouble with the law; they also provide the old and sick with adequate medical and other care. Still, throughout Europe, these government measures are the exception rather than the rule, and even in the Netherlands, Sinti Gypsies are quick to blame the Romany newcomers for anti-Gypsy attitudes. One Sinti stated, "The newcomers are responsible for our unpopularity. I sometimes meet them, but can't talk to them—we speak Sinti with a lot of Dutch words; they speak something different."[42]

The average German citizen also continues to be aware of the Gypsies' "separateness," as the following examples show. In February 1993, a woman of German ethnicity, who is now an American citizen, returned to Germany to visit her sister. She related the following:

> My sister has a Gasthaus in a small town near Berlin. It is quite a nice place, and she does a good business. But always, she has to be on the caution for Gypsies. They come and stay, and she cannot turn them away without getting into some little trouble.

Asked if the Gypsies caused any problems to her sister or the other guests, the woman shrugged and said, "No. But you know how they are. Gypsies—they hang around the place in a large group. It doesn't look good. They speak differently; they do not mix; they are always keeping only to themselves."

An American businessman who was in Bonn in August 1993 told of driving his German friends about the city. Apparently, he was not too familiar with the area, and as he made a rather sharp turn, he nearly hit a pedestrian. When he expressed his relief at having missed the walker, one of his friends commented, "Oh, don't worry. It's only a Gypsy. They are not really one of us."

Integration into a host society—one of the conditions originally required in Hamburg and also one of the chief aims of the programs in Holland—continues to be an almost insurmountable problem for Gypsy and Gaje alike. Gypsies wish to retain their centuries of tradition; the Gaje demand assimilation. Many Gypsies continue to live free, taking what they need from the land or the surrounding communities; the Gaje jail them for theft. Those Gypsies who have become more assimilated into the host societies resent the wandering Roma, whose traditional ways arouse continual prejudice toward all Gypsies. A common ground for the Roma and the Gaje will be difficult to find, but some on both sides are now attempting to solve the problems which have existed for centuries.

SOME INTERNATIONAL SUPPORT

In the past few years, a few Gypsies have become actively engaged in a battle to inform the world of the tragedy which befell them during the holocaust and to demand that they no longer suffer humiliation, discrimination, and, possibly, death at the hands of Gaje society. Support is coming not only from Gypsy groups but from other concerned people and organizations as well. Included in the organizations worldwide are: the International Romani Union, the Gypsy Lore Society, UNICEF, the United Nations, the Organization for Threatened Societies, the Commission for Racial Equality, the Romani Anti-Defamation League, the Roma and Sinti Union, the National Gypsy Education Council (London), and the newly formed Romani-Jewish Alliance.

For example, the United States Congressional Caucus on Human Rights protested "the forced sterilization of Gypsy women, and the permanent removal of their children for placement in government homes."[43] Newsletters from the Gypsy Lore Society keep people informed of continuing Gypsy problems in Europe and the United States, while the organization Human Rights Watch has denounced treatment of European Gypsies. Press releases from the Romani Union and the Romani-Jewish Alliance update the public on various outrageous acts perpetrated on Gypsies.

One of the major issues fought for by the Romani Union was inclusion in the Holocaust Memorial Museum in the United States—a museum to be funded through tax-deductible contributions. Ian Hancock, professor in the departments of English and Linguistics at the University of Texas in Austin, was appointed to represent the world's 8 million Gypsies at the United Nations. Hancock charged in 1984 that officials of the Holocaust Memorial Council (which was established by Congress in 1980 with an $800,000 annual budget and charged with planning a museum to the 11 million holocaust victims) had ignored correspondence from UN delegates and leaders of the World Romani Union. Pointing out that the Gypsies were the *first* victims of the holocaust in Europe, Hancock charged discrimination against Gypsies from Jewish leaders of the council.[44]

Hancock was particularly upset that no Gypsies had ever been approached by the sixty-five members of the U.S. Holocaust Memorial Council regarding their experiences. In a *Report for the Holocaust Memorial Commission to the President of the United States*, Elie Wiesel (Jewish author and recipient of the Nobel Peace Prize) claimed that the holocaust was "essentially a Jewish event.... [T]he Jewish people alone were destined to be totally annihilated...." The word "Gypsy" appeared only once in the document—in an appendix. Professor Seymour Seigel, a former chairman of the Holocaust Memorial Council, questioned in a *Washington Post* article whether the Gypsies were actually a separate ethnic group and called the Gypsies' attempts to gain recognition "cockamamie." Gypsy protestors were also labeled "cranks" and "eccentrics."[45]

However, Hancock found help for his cause from a number of holocaust scholars who began to present information on the extermination of the Gypsies. Then, in a December 1984, letter to Elie Wiesel, Simon Wiesenthal protested the exclusion of the Gypsies from the Memorial

Council, writing that "the Gypsies had been murdered [in a proportion] similar to the Jews; about 80 per cent of them in the area of the countries which were occupied by the Nazis."[46]

Hancock's efforts and the efforts of others were finally successful, and in 1987 William Duna, a Rom, was appointed to the Holocaust Memorial Council. Now the Gypsies are included in the memorial as victims of this infamous era. Still, a four-page article in a 1993 issue of *Newsweek*, dealing with the new United States Holocaust Memorial Museum, mentions the word "Gypsies" only once—lumping them into a category of "5 million others" exterminated by the Nazis. The impression is still given that the Gypsies in their own right are not worth mentioning.[47]

In Europe the furor over inclusion in memorials continues. A holocaust memorial has been proposed for Berlin, but Ignatz Bubis of the Zentralrat der Juden in Deutschland stated in 1993 that the organization did not wish to have Gypsy suffering acknowledged on the same memorial with the Jews. In fact, they did not want a Gypsy memorial anywhere near to the Jewish memorial. Oskar Rose, a Gypsy activist in Germany, was in Berlin in November 1993 to protest the exclusion of Gypsies. Rose felt that there should be one memorial for all holocaust victims, regardless of their race, ethnic background, or religion. After learning of Rose's comments, Bubis relented somewhat—still opting for a separate Jewish memorial but indicating that a Gypsy memorial, with similar architecture, could be constructed nearby.

So, the saga of the "Gypsy problem" continues. For most of the Romany in Europe, the decades prior to World War II and the hell of the holocaust appear little different from the decades following the war. The repressive laws, beatings, deportations throughout Europe, and recent border closing in Germany all affect this persecuted minority today as they have in the past. Perhaps Association of Parish Councils in Hampshire, England, was correct in saying, "They are a people without hope." The Gypsies do not belong to the past or the present—and who can predict their future?

Epilogue

෬

ALTHOUGH LIFE IN THE United States is much better than life in Europe for the Roma, there is still a great deal of prejudice against the Gypsies. Frequently, editorials, news stories, and cartoons which portray a negative image of Gypsies as an ethnic group appear in national newspapers and magazines. The stereotype of the thieving Gypsy is ever present. In 1983 an article appeared in a police magazine stating, "The only measure of respect that a Gypsy woman can get is based on her abilities as a thief." A Michigan Detective Sergeant defined Gypsies as "domineering, very loud, cunning... completely comfortable with a lifestyle centered around victimizing others.[1] An October 1993 newspaper in Colorado carried a Halloween story for children in which a young girl reminisces about a visit with her grandmother:

> "The Gypsies" was this week's topic. She told me in her old and crackly Sicilian voice, "Lisa, you better watch out for the gypsies!" I asked her who the gypsies were and why I should watch out for them. Granny said they're people who hide and then suddenly take you for everything you have....[2]

Think of the repercussions if such comments were published about Blacks, Hispanics, or some other ethnic minority in the U.S.

In some states, anti-Gypsy statutes—old laws which should have been removed long ago—are still on the books. New York and Chicago have special police assigned to the Rom. In many small towns across America, sheriffs or their deputies escort Gypsies to the county line.[3]

Not too many years ago, in Maryland, a family was arrested for refusing to pay the $1,000 yearly fee for a license which permits a Gypsy to "establish a homesite" in Montgomery County. There is a $10 bounty, payable to the officer who makes the arrest, on the head of any Gypsy who hasn't paid the fee.[4] Whether or not these laws are always strictly enforced, they are there—a reminder that Gypsies were and are unwelcome.

With the renewed publicity in America about the holocaust period, one would assume that the Gypsies would get equal representation for their victimization and that the decimation of their numbers would be an accepted fact. However, this is not the case. In April 1993, the Holocaust Memorial Museum was dedicated in Washington, DC Articles written about this museum remind the public that the memorial is "...remembering...the six million Jews who perished in the Holocaust." The extermination of up to 1 million Gypsies is only briefly noted in passing and lumped together with any other victims—"The murder of ten of thousands of Gypsies, Poles, and other innocent people."[5] At this monument, whose stated purpose is to make sure that the world does not forget these crimes against humanity, the Gypsies are given little importance.

Also, there are still some who choose to disparage documentation of holocaust deaths. For example, a July 1994 letter to *National Geographic* criticizes a previously published article in which the magazine cites an American airman who indicated that 1,300 Gypsy children aged six to ten were killed by the Germans at Buchenwald. "This is hearsay and an outright lie," the writer from Jamestown, Michigan, states. "No country or people in the world would do a thing like that."[6]

And, today in Europe, concentration camps for minorities or political prisoners are on the rise once again in the Balkans. Daily, the press presents to the viewing public the atrocities; politicians debate the charges of ethnic cleansing; diplomats strive ineffectively to free camp prisoners; as when they visited Auschwitz in the 1940s, Red Cross officials inspecting the camps today deny any "wrong doing" exists. Is history repeating itself?

Appendix One

Nazi Concentration Camps

To AID THE READER, following is a listing of the major concentration camps, together with their date of construction and original purpose. Records vary as to their size, purpose, number and ethnicity of inmates, and death count.

AUSCHWITZ-BIRKENAU. Erected 1940 in southwestern Poland as a camp for Polish prisoners of war. Converted, end of 1941 / early 1942 into modern facility for extermination. Camp was a complex of sites—Buna, Monowitz, and original Auschwitz housed slave laborers for construction and industry. Birkenau was annihilation site. (Estimates of those killed in this center: two to four million.) Liberated by Soviet troops in January 1945.

BELZEC. Erected March 1942 in eastern Poland. Known as a "killing center." Dismantled by Nazis in the fall of 1943.

BERGEN-BELSEN. Erected 1943 in northwestern Germany. Liberated by British troops in April 1945.

BUCHENWALD. Erected 1937 near Weimar in central Germany for German political prisoners. Satellites included Bernburg and Lauenburg. Thousands of prisoners died there. Liberated in April 1945 by inmates a few hours before arrival of American troops.

CHELMNO. Established 1941 in western Poland. First Nazi extermination camp, using carbon monoxide gas vans. Dismantled by Nazis in late 1944/ early 1945.

DACHAU. First Nazi concentration camp, erected 1933 near Munich, mainly for German political prisoners. In late 1938 Jews, Gypsies, Jehovah's Witnesses, homosexuals, and other "asocial" elements were sent there. Many prisoners used as guinea pigs in experiments. Gas chamber at Dachau never operational. Satellites included Oberdorf, Obertaufkirchen, Burgau. Liberated in April 1945 by American troops.

FLOSSENBERG. Erected in 1938 in central Germany (near Floss in eastern Bavarian woods) specifically for slave labor in stone quarries. Prior to liberation in April 1945 by American troops, Nazis had forced 15,000 to 20,000 prisoners on a "death march" away from the camp.

JASENOVAC. In Yugoslavia approximately 120 miles north of Sarajevo. 700,000 of all nationalities (including Gypsies) died here.

MAJDANEK (ALSO CALLED LUBLIN). Established late 1941/early 1942, originally for Soviet POWs and civilian prisoners. Converted to "killing center." Liberated by Soviet troops in 1944.

MAUTHAUSEN. Erected 1938 near Linz, Austria, for slave labor. Satellites included Ebensee, Wels. Thousands later gassed before liberation by American troops in May 1945.

NEUENGAMME. Erected June 1940 in northern Germany, principally as a center of slave labor for industries in that area. Satellites included Lerbeck, Woebbelin. Many prisoners died of malnutrition/disease before liberation by British troops in May 1945.

NORDHAUSEN (ALSO CALLED DORA). Established 1943 in central Germany. Slave laborers in production of V-1 flying bombs and V-2 rockets. Liberated by American troops in April 1945.

ORANIENBURG. Established 1933 in northern Germany for political prisoners. Ceased operating 1935 but was reopened in 1943 as a satellite of

Sachsenhausen. Liberated April 1945 by Soviet troops and units of the Polish People's Army.

RAVENSBRÜCK. Established in 1939 near Berlin, exclusively for female prisoners. Liberated in April 1945 by Soviet troops.

SACHSENHAUSEN. Established 1936 near Berlin. Liberated by Soviet troops in April 1945.

SOBIBOR. Established in 1942 in eastern Poland as extermination camp. Hundreds of thousands died there. Dismantled by Nazis in the fall of 1943.

THERESIENSTADT (TEREZIN). Established in 1941 in northwestern Czechoslovakia. Served for a period of time as a Nazi "show camp" for visiting Red Cross inspectors. Liberated by Soviet troops in May 1945.

TREBLINKA. Established 1942 in central Poland as an extermination camp. Over 750,000 died there. Nazis dismantled the camp in the fall of 1943.

WARSAW GHETTO. Created in 1940. In 1942 deportations began for extermination, mainly at Treblinka.

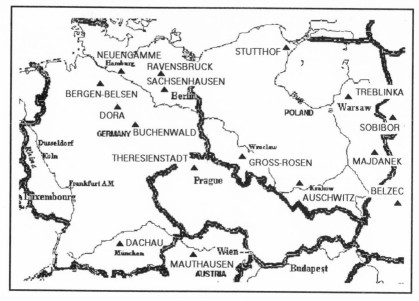

Concentration Camps, 1933–1945

Classification of Gypsies in Germany at Outbreak of World War II

THIS INFORMATION IS TAKEN from *The Destiny of Europe's Gypsies*, pp. 84–86.

Lalleri. Also, Lalleri Sinti ("dumb" Gypsies who speak a different dialect) thought to be a branch of the "German Sinti" but linguistically a subgroup of the Rom.

Litautikker. Were sedentary in East Prussia; probably a subgroup of the Sinti but not classed as such by Ritter.

Rom. Had come to Germany from Hungary in mid-1800s.

Sinti. Had come as early as the fifteenth century (could be called native to Germany). Name may come from the province of Sind in India. Sinti Gypsies were to be noted as "Native Gypsies."

OTHERS
Kelderari, Lovari, Drisari, Medvashi in Yugoslavia; also those known as Balkan Gypsies in Burgenland.

A further refinement was set up in August 1941, into pure and part-Gypsies:

Z	pure Gypsy (*Zigeuner*)
ZM+, ZM(+)	more than half-Gypsy
ZM	part-Gypsy (*Zigeunermischling*)
ZM 1st grade	half-Gypsy, half-German
ZM 2nd grade	half-ZM I, half-German
AM-, ZM(-)	more than half-German
NZ	non-Gypsy (*Nicht-Zigeuner*)

As Dr. Ritter explained, the classification was not based entirely on genealogy. He divided Gypsies into pure and mixed on the following grounds.

1. General impression and physical appearance.
2. Belonging to a Romany-speaking community.
3. Links with tribal laws.
4. Gypsy way of life.
5. Genealogy (which seemed to be of prime importance when decisions were made on who would be taken to Auschwitz).

Notes

∾

Chapter One: Centuries of Persecution

1 Jean-Pierre Liegeois, *Gypsies: An Illustrated History*, trans. Tony Berrett (London: Al Saqi Books, 1986), 19-24.
2 Judith Okely, *The Traveller Gypsies* (Cambridge: Cambridge University Press, 1983), 3.
3 Brian Vesey-Fitzgerald, *Gypsies of Britain: An Introduction to Their History* (London: Chapman and Hale, 1944), 13-28.
4 Okely, *Traveller Gypsies*, 4.
5 Jan Yoors, *The Gypsies* (New York: Simon and Schuster, 1967), 9; Bart McDowell, *Gypsies: Wanderers of the World* (Washington, D.C., National Geographic Society, 1970), 190.
6 McDowell, *Gypsies: Wanderers*, 186-189.
7 Ibid., 23; Gabrielle Tyrnauer, *Gypsies and the Holocaust: A Bibliography and Introductory Essay*, (Montreal: Centre Interuniversitaire D'etudes Europeennes, 1989), viii.
8 McDowell, *Gypsies: Wanderers*, 187.
9 Tyrnauer, *Gypsies and the Holocaust*, viii-ix.
10 Donald Kenrick and Grattan Puxon, *The Destiny of Europe's Gypsies* (London: Chatto-Heinemann for Sussex University Press, 1972), 15.
11 Ian Hancock, *The Pariah Syndrome: An Account of Gypsy Slavery and Persecution* (Ann Arbor, Mich.: Karoma, 1987), 11-15.
12 Liegeois, *Gypsies: Illustrated History*, 110.
13 Ibid., 89.
14 Hancock, *Pariah Syndrome*, 58-59.; Liegeois, *Gypsies: Illustrated History*, 88-89.
15 Liegeois, *Gypsies: Illustrated History*, 107.
16 Ibid., 106-110.
17 Ibid., 88-89.
18 Kenrick and Puxon, *Destiny of Europe's Gypsies*, 19.
19 Jean Paul Clebert, *Gypsies*, trans. Charles Duff (New York: Penguin, 1967), 55.

20 Kenrick and Puxon, *Destiny of Europe's Gypsies*, 55.
21 Ibid., 24–25.
22 Ibid., 25.
23 McDowell, *Gypsies: Wanderers*, 160.
24 Yoors, *Gypsies*, 9.
25 McDowell, *Gypsies: Wanderers*, 14–15.
26 Kenrick and Puxon, *Destiny of Europe's Gypsies*, 26–27.
27 Walter Starkie, *In Sara's Tents* (New York: E. P. Dutton, 1953), 43.
28 Hancock, *Pariah Syndrome*, 53.
29 Kenrick and Puxon, *Destiny of Europe's Gypsies*, 28.
30 Ibid., 28.
31 Ibid., 22.
32 Nebojsa Bato Tomasevic and Rajko Djuric, *Gypsies of the World* (London: Flint River Press, 1988), 9.
33 Yoors, *Gypsies*, 110–111.
34 Dora Yates, "Hitler and the Gypsies," *Commentary* (American Jewish Committee) 8 (November 1949), 456.
35 Tyrnauer, *Gypsies and the Holocaust*, xi.
36 Kenrick and Puxon, *Destiny of Europe's Gypsies*, 55–56.
37 Ibid., 50–56.

CHAPTER TWO: OMINOUS SIGNS

1 Gabriel Tyrnauer, *Gypsies and the Holocaust, A Bibliography and Introductory Essay* (Montreal: Centre Interuniversitaire D'Etudes Europeennes, 1989), xii, xiii.
2 Donald Kenrick and Grattan Puxon, *The Destiny of Europe's Gypsies* (London: Chatto-Heinemann for Sussex University Press, 1972), 59–60.
3 *Die Judenfrage* (Vertrauliche Beilage), April 15, 1942, 30–31.
4 Kenrick and Puxon, *Destiny of Europe's Gypsies*, 59.
5 Philip Friedman, "The Extermination of the Gypsies, A Nazi Genocide Operation Against an Aryan People," *Jewish Frontier* (January 1951).
6 Nora Levin, *The Holocaust: The Destruction of European Jewry, 1933–1945* (New York: Schocken Books, 1990), 668; Freidman, *Extermination of the Gypsies*.
7 Kenrick and Puxon, *Destiny of Europe's Gypsies*, 59.
8 Sybil Milton, "The Context of the Holocaust," *German Studies Review* 13, no. 2 (May 1990), 270–271; Ian Hancock, remarks at the Day of Remembrance in Memory of the Gypsy Victims of Nazi Genocide, United States Memorial Council, Washington, D.C., 1980.
9 Ibid., 271.
10 Tilman Zülch, *In Auschwitz vergast, bis heute verfolgt: zur Situation der Roma (Zigeuner) in Deutschland und Europa* (Reinbeck bei Hamburg: Rowohlt, 1979), 156.
11 Milton, *"Context of the Holocaust,"* 271–273.
12 Tyrnauer, *Gypsies and the Holocaust*, xi.
13 Kenrick and Puxon, *Destiny of Europe's Gypsies*, 57.
14 Ibid., 57–58.
15 Ibid., 70.
16 Donald Kenrick and Gratton Puxon, *Sinti und Roma, die Vernichtung eines Volkes im NS-Staat*,

trans. Astrid Stegelmann (London: Chatto-Heinemann-Sussex, 1972), 56.
17 Benno Muller-Hill, *Murderous Science: Elimination by Scientific Selection of Jews, Gypsies, and others, Germany 1933-1945*, trans. George R. Fraser (Oxford: Oxford University Press, 1988), 57.
18 *Encyclopedia of the Holocaust*, 2:635.
19 Kenrick and Puxon, *Destiny of Europe's Gypsies*, 68.
20 Muller-Hill, *Murderous Science*, 58.
21 Joachim S. Hohmann, *Verfolgte ohne Heimat: Geschichte der Zigeuner in Deutschland*, trans. Andrew Pollinger (Frankfurt am Main: Peter Lang, 1990), 172.
22 Ludwig Eiber, *Ich wusste es wird schlimm: Die Verfolgung der Sinti und Roma in München 1933-1945* (München: Buchendorfer Verlag, 1993), 47.
23 Tilman Zülch, *In Auschwitz vergast*, 75-76.
24 Ibid., 163.
25 Eiber, *Ich wusste*, 49.
26 Rudolph Blank and Jurgen Roth, "Zigeuner Leben: Über ein Dasein zwischen Romantik und Wirklichkeit," from the German television program *Reportage am Montag* (ZDF), Fall 1985.
27 Bart McDowell, *Gypsies: Wanderers of the World* (Washington D.C.: National Georgraphic Society, 1970), 65.
28 Kenrick and Puxon, *Sinti und Roma*, 75.
29 Ibid., 76.
30 Ibid., 76.; Zülch, *In Auschwitz vergast, bis Heute verfolgt*, 80.
31 Bohdan Wytwycky, "The Plight of the Gypsies,"in *The Other Holocaust: Many Circles of Hell* (Washington, D.C.: Novak Report on the New Ethnicity, 1980), 124.
32 Kenrick and Puxon, *Destiny of Europe's Gypsies*, 60-61.
33 Philip Friedman, "Extermination of the Gypsies."

Chapter Three: A Deadly Journey

1 Tilman Zülch, *In Auschwitz vergast, bis heute verfolgt: zur Situation der Roma (Zigeuner) in Deutschland und Europa* (Reinbeck bei Hamburg: Rowohlt, 1979), 81.
2 Donald Kenrick and Grattan Puxon, *The Destiny of Europe's Gypsies* (London: Chatto-Heinemann for Sussex University Press, 1972), 78.
3 Raul Hilberg, *The Destruction of the European Jews* (Chicago: Quadrangle Books, 1961), 641.
4 Miriam Novitch, "Romani Genocide Under the Nazi Regime" (1968), 10-11.
5 Ibid., 10-12.
6 All material on Lena Winterstein from videotape: Rudolph Blank and Jurgen Roth, "Zigeuner Leben: Über ein Dasein zwischen Romantik und Wirklichkeit," from the German television program *Reportage am Montag* (ZDF), Fall 1985.
7 All material on Wanda G. is from personal correspondence and court records. This individual wishes to remain anonymous as she still lives in and has family in Germany.
8 Kenrick and Puxon, *Destiny of Europe's Gypsies*, 101-102.
9 Nora Levin, *The Holocaust: The Destruction of European Jewry, 1933-1945* (New York: Schocken Books, 1990), 431.
10 Kenrick and Puxon, *Destiny of Europe's Gypsies*, 102-103.
11 Ibid., 103.
12 Ibid., 103-106.

13 Ibid., 106.
14 Ibid., 106.
15 Ibid., 108.
16 Ibid., 100-101.
17 Yitzhak Arad, *Belzec, Sobibor, Treblinka: The Operation Reinhard Death Camps* (Bloomington: Indiana University Press, 1987), 153.
18 Levin, *The Holocaust*, 244.
19 *Encyclopedia of the Holocaust*, 2:637.
20 Novitch, *Romani Genocide*, 13.
21 Levin, *The Holocaust*, 668.
22 Jerzy Ficowski, *Gypsies on Polish Roads*, 3d ed., trans. Regina Gelb (Krakow-Wroclaw: Wydawnectwo Literackie, 1985), 129-130; 137.
23 Kenrick and Puxon, *Destiny of Europe's Gypsies*, 130.
24 Ibid., 131-133.
34 Bohdan Wytwycky, "The Plight of the Gypsies,"in *The Other Holocaust: Many Circles of Hell* (Washington, D.C.: Novak Report on the New Ethnicity, 1980), 125.
1 Levin, *The Holocaust*, 514-515.
2 Edmond Paris, *Genocide in Satellite Croatia, 1941-1945: A Record of Racial and Religious Persecutions and Massacres*, trans. Lois Perkins (Chicago: American Institute for Balkan Affairs, 1961), 62.
3 Levin, *The Holocaust*, 515.
4 Ibid., 668; Ficowski, *Gypsies on Polish Roads*, 25; Kenrick and Puxon, *Destiny of Europe's Gypsies*, 114.
5 Novitch, *Romani Genocide*, 13.
6 Primo Levi, *The Drowned and the Saved*, trans. Raymond Rosenthal (New York: Summit Books, 1988), 69.
7 Alexander Ramati, *And the Violins Stopped Playing: A Story of the Gypsy Holocaust* (New York: Franklin Watts, 1986), 167-168.
8 Ibid., 169.
9 Ibid., 171-172.
10 Ibid., 171-174.
11 All material on Katja Z. is from an interview of January 6, 1991. The name of this interviewee was changed as she wishes to remain anonymous for fear of persecution to her family.
12 Comments by Francis P. (New York) from a telephone interview, December 1994.
13 Telephone interview with David P., Brooklyn, N.Y. (January 6, 1995)
14 J. Frank Diggs, *The Welcome Swede* (New York: Vantage Press, 1988), 119-120. Mr. Soderberg also discussed this incident with one of the authors in Colorado Springs in 1993.
15 Philip Friedman, "The Extermination of the Gypsies, A Nazi Genocide Operation Against an Aryan People," *Jewish Frontier* (January 1951); Kenrick and Puxon, *Destiny of Europe's Gypsies*, 109.
16 Ibid., 79-80.
17 Ibid., 106.
18 Bart McDowell, *Gypsies: Wanderers of the World* (Washington, D.C., National Geographic Society, 1970), 63.

CHAPTER FOUR: THE EFFORT OF SURVIVAL

1   Rudolph Höss, *Death Dealer: The Memoirs of the SS Kommandant at Auschwitz*, ed. Steven Paskuly (Buffalo, N.Y.: Prometheus Books, 1992), 136.
2   Bart McDowell, *Gypsies: Wanderers of the World* (Washington, D.C., National Geographic Society, 1970).
3   Donald Kenrick and Grattan Puxon, *The Destiny of Europe's Gypsies* (London: Chatto-Heinemann for Sussex University Press, 1972), 155.
4   Alexander Ramati, *And the Violins Stopped Playing: A Story of the Gypsy Holocaust* (New York: Franklin Watts, 1986), 195.
5   Höss, *Death Dealer*, 136.
6   Philip Friedman, "The Extermination of the Gypsies, A Nazi Genocide Operation Against an Aryan People," *Jewish Frontier* (January 1951), 13.
7   Lucjan Dobroszycki, ed. *The Chronicle of the Lodz Ghetto, 1941–1944*, trans. Richard Lourie, et al. (New Haven: Yale University Press, 1984), 101; 107–108.
8   Ibid., 85–86.
9   Ibid., 86.
10 Rudolph Blank and Jurgen Roth, "Zigeuner Leben: Über ein Dasein zwischen Romantik und Wirklichkeit," from the German television program *Reportage am Montag* (ZDF), Fall 1985.
11 Joachim S. Hohmann, *Verfolgte ohne heimat: Geschichte der Zigeuner in Deutschland*, trans. Andrew Pollinger (Frankfurt am Main: Peter Lang, 1990), 178.
12 From Düsseldorf court records.
13 Eugen Kogon, *The Theory and Practice of Hell* (London: Secker and Warburg, 1976), 102.

CHAPTER FIVE: GYPSY GENOCIDE

1   Tilman Zülch, *In Auschwitz vergast, bis heute verfolgt: zur Situation der Roma (Zigeuner) in Deutschland und Europa* (Reinbeck bei Hamburg: Rowohlt, 1979), 104.; Donald Kenrick and Grattan Puxon, *The Destiny of Europe's Gypsies* (London: Chatto-Heinemann for Sussex University Press, 1972), 165.
2   Zülch, *In Auschwitz vergast*, 104.
3   Benno Muller-Hill, *Murderous Science: Elimination by Scientific Selection of Jews, Gypsies, and Others, Germany 1933–1945*, trans. George R. Fraser (Oxford: Oxford University Press, 1988), 60.
4   Ian Hancock, *The Pariah Syndrome* (Ann Arbor, Mich.: Karoma, 1987), 81.
5   Zülch, *In Auschwitz vergast*, 105.
6   Primo Levi, *The Drowned and the Saved*, trans. Raymond Rosenthal (New York: Summit Books, 1988), 119.
7   Jerzy Ficowski, *Gypsies on Polish Roads*, 3d ed., trans. Regina Gelb (Krakow-Wroclaw: Sydawnictwo Literackie, 1985), 46.
8   Zulch, *In Auschwitz vergast*, 105.
9   Kenrick and Puxon, *The Destiny of Europe's Gypsies*, 163–164.
10 Jerzy Ficowski, *The Gypsies in Poland: History and Customs* (Warsaw: Interpress Publishers, 1989), 48.
11 Kenrick and Puxon, *The Destiny of Europe's Gypsies*, 165.
12 Ficowski, *Gypsies on Polish Roads*, 16–17.

13 Helen Davis, "Angels of Life," *Hadassah Magazine* (November 1985), 23.; Martin Gilbert, *The Holocaust: A History of the Jews of Europe during the Second World War* (New York: Holt, Rhinehart and Winston, 1985), 689.
14 Ficowski, *Gypsies on Polish Roads*, 16.
15 Gabrielle Tyrnauer, "'Uncle Mengele' dispensed candy, death to Gypsy children," *The Montreal Gazette* (June 15, 1985).
16 Ficowski, *Gypsies on Polish Roads*, 16.
17 Ina R. Friedman, *The Other Victims: First-Person Stories of Non-Jews Persecuted by the Nazis* (Boston: Houghton Mifflin, 1990), 10.
18 Viktor E. Frankl, *Man's Search for Meaning: An Introduction to Logotherapy* (New York: Simon and Schuster, 1984), 40.
19 Ficowski, *Gypsies on Polish Roads*, 16.
20 Zulch, *In Auschwitz vergast*, 134.
21 Kenrick and Puxon, *The Destiny of Europe's Gypsies*, 159.
22 Ibid., 157.
23 Höss, *Death Dealer*, 137.
24 Alexander Ramati, *And the Violins Stopped Playing: A Story of the Gypsy Holocaust* (New York: Franklin Watts, 1986), 193–194.
25 Ibid., 197.
26 Yitzhak Arad, *Belzec, Sobibor, Treblinka: The Operation Reinhard Death Camps* (Bloomington: Indiana University Press, 1987), 152.
27 Jacob Wiernik, *A Yor in Treblinka*, (New York: 1944), 51–52.
28 This material is again cited because of the discrepancies found in sources. Some indicate the Lodz Gypsies died from natural causes (see chapter 4); others indicate the Lodz Gypsies were "exterminated."
29 Ficowski, *Gypsies on Polish Roads*, 1–2.
30 Ibid., 3–5.
31 Arad, *Belsec, Sobibor, Treblinka*, 151.
32 Hancock, *Pariah Syndrome*, 68–70.
33 Gilbert, *The Holocaust*, 250–251.
34 Arad, *Belsec, Sobibor, Treblinka*, 152.
35 Kenrick and Puxon, *The Destiny of Europe's Gypsies*, 168–169.
36 Eugen Kogon, *The Theory and Practice of Hell* (London: Secker and Warburg, 1976), 47.
37 Gilbert, *The Holocuast*, 259–260.
38 Ibid., 260.
39 Kenrick and Puxon, *The Destiny of Europe's Gypsies*, 180.
40 Kogon, *The Theory and Practice of Hell*, 129.
41 It is difficult to arrive at a firm figure for the number of Gypsy victims of the holocaust because sources vary greatly in their estimates. For example: In *The Pariah Syndrome*, Ian Hancock gives a figure of 600,000 Gypsy dead, while in a 1988 article in *The EAFORD International Review of Racial Discrimination* entitled "'Uniqueness' of the Victims: Gypsies, Jews, and the Holocaust," he indicates "the Nazis killed between a fourth and third of the Gypsies living in Europe, and as many as 70 per cent in those areas where Nazi control had been established longest." Gabrielle Tyrnauer, *Gypsies and the Holocaust*, estimates the murder of between a quarter and a half million Gypsies, approximately a fourth of all those living in prewar Europe. Bohdan Wytwycky, "The Plight of the Gypsies," states that in Estonia "the annihilation of the Gypsy population is estimated to have been complete,"

and at the Babi Yar ravine in Russia "entire camps of Gypsies were led to Babi Yar." The estimates of Simon Wiesenthal and Miriam Novitch are higher yet.

42 Simon Wiesenthal, *Justice n'est pas vengeance: Une autobiographie*, (Paris: Editions Robert Laffont, 1989), 394.

43 Ian Hancock, "Fate of Hitler's Romani (Gypsy) victims yet to become part of Holocaust history," *The Detroit Jewish News*, 8.

CHAPTER SIX: FREE AT LAST

1   Karl Stojka, *The Story of Karl Stojka: A Childhood in Birkenau*, Exhibition at the embassy of Austria, April 30 to May 29, 1992 (Washington, D.C.: United States Holocaust Memorial Council, 1992), 52.

2   Martin Gilbert, *The Holocaust: A History of the Jews of Europe during the Second World War* (New York: Holt, Rhinehart and Winston, 1985), 795.

3   Donald Kenrick and Grattan Puxon, *The Destiny of Europe's Gypsies* (London: Chatto-Heinemann for Sussex University Press, 1972), 187.

4   Brewster Chamberlin and Marcia Feldman, eds. *The Liberation of the Nazi Concentration Camps, 1945: Eyewitness Accounts of the Liberators*, (Washington, D.C.: United States Holocaust Memorial Council, 1987), 76.

5   Peter Lyon, *Eisenhower: Portrait of the Hero*, (Boston: Little, Brown, 1974), 338.

6   Martin Blumenson, *Patton: The Man behind the Legend, 1885-1945*, (New York: William Morrow, 1985), 264.

7   Ibid., 264.

8   Dwight D. Eisenhower, *Letters to Mamie*, ed. John S. D. Eisenhower (Garden City, N.Y.: Doubleday, 1978), 248.

9   Dwight D. Eisenhower, *The Papers of Dwight David Eisenhower*, ed. Alfred D. Chandler, Jr. (Baltimore: Johns Hopkins Press, 1970), 2616. Similar comments are also cited in Chamberlin and Feldman, *Liberation of the Nazi Concentration Camps*, 76-77.; Stephen E. Ambrose, *The Supreme Commander* (New York: Doubleday, 1970), 659.; idem, *Eisenhower: Soldier, General of the Army, President Elect, 1890-1952* (New York: Simon and Schuster, 1983), 400.)

10 Eisenhower, *Papers*, 2623.

11 Ambrose, *Supreme Commander*, 659.

12 Chamberlin and Feldman, *Liberation of theNazi Concentration Camps*, 152.

13 There is much confusion in this account. Ramati states that he was the *last* Gypsy left in Auschwitz, after the extermination of all Gypsies in Auschitz-Birkenau in 1944. Other accounts indicate that there were several Gypsies left among the Jews in Auschwitz. Ramati also states that he escaped from Auschwitz.

14 Alexander Ramati, *And the Violins Stopped Playing: A Story of the Gypsy Holocaust* (New York: Franklin Watts, 1986), 236-237.

15 Interview with Dolores Zimmermann Randerson, daughter of Dr. Zimmermann, June 1994.

16 Gilbert, *Holocaust*, 795.

17 Stojka, *Story of Karl Stojka*, 11.

18 Jean-Pierre Liegeois, *Gypsies: An Illustrated History*, trans. Tony Berrett (London: Al Saqi Books, 1986), 93.

19 Kenrick and Puxon, *Destiny of Europe's Gypsies*, 188.

20 Ibid., 189.

CHAPTER SEVEN: THE "GYPSY PROBLEM" CONTINUES

1 Janos Kenedi, "Why is the Gypsy the Scapegoat and not the Jew?" *East European Reporter* (1986): 11.
2 *The Romani-Jewish Alliance Newsletter* (February –March 1993), 2.
3 Ibid., 1.
4 Interview with Siegfried and Ophelia T. These were friends of Katja H. who visited her in Colorado in 1992.
5 Robert Fisk, "Fear of Nazis reigns among Vienna gypsies 50 years on," *New York Times* (March 14, 1988).
6 Ian Hancock, "Gypsies: A People Forgotten," *The Humanist* (September/October 1985), 12.
7 *Trials of War Criminals before the Nürnberg Military Tribunals under Control Council Law No. 10.* Vol. 4 (Washington, D.C.: U.S. Government Printing Office), 286.
8 Ibid., 286-287.
9 Ibid., 418-427.
10 Ibid., 503.
11 Simon Wiesenthal, *Justice n'est pas vengeance: Une Autobiographie* (Paris: Editions Robert Laffont, 1989), 2.
12 Thomas Acton, *Gypsy Politics and Social Change: The Development of Ethnic Ideology and Pressure Politics among British Gypsies from Victorian Reformism to Romany Nationalism* (London: Routledge and Kegal Paul, 1974), 191-194.
13 Hancock, "Gypsies," 15.
14 Nebojsa Bato Tomasevic and Rajko Djuric, *Gypsies of the World* (London: Flint River Press, 1988), 281.
15 Letter from Spanish and Portuguese Jews' Congregation, London, to Mr. Hayton, Essex County Council, Chelmsford, Essex, 7 December 1987; rebuttal letter from Yanko le Redzosko, Secretary, Romani Union, Buda, Texas, 25 July 1988; reply to Redzosko from Spanish and Portuguese Jews' Congregation, 9 August 1988.
16 "Anti-Gypsy Prejudice Rages in England," *The Romani-Jewish Alliance Newsletter* (September–October 1993): 6.
17 *The Romani-Jewish Alliance Newsletter* (April, 1995): 3; from *Searchlight* (March 1995)
18 Bogumila Michalewicz, "ctives perspectivespersp," *Newsletter of the North American Chapter of the Gypsy Lore Society* (Summer 1982).
19 Tomasevic and Djuric, *Gypsies of the World.*
20 "Anti-Gypsy Action in France," *The Romani-Jewish Alliance Newsletter* (September–October 1993): 5.
21 Ian Hancock, "The Plight of the Romani Children, " *Action for Children* (NGO committee on UNICEF) , no. 3 (1987).
22 Rachel Tritt, *Struggling for Ethnic Identity: Czechoslovakia's Endangered Gypsies* (New York: Human Rights Watch, 1992), 114.
23 "Prague Against Gypsies," *Insight* (September 15, 1986): 40.
24 "Czechoslovakia Harsh on Its Gypsy Population," *Insight* (September 7, 1987): 27.
25 Press release, Romani Union, Manchaco, Texas, April, 1990.
26 Tritt, *Struggling for Ethnic Identity*, 22-23.
27 Ibid., 29-34.
28 Kenedi, "Why is the Gypsy the Scapegoat and not the Jew?," 11.
29 Tomasevic and Djuric, *Gypsies of the World*, 184.

30 Tilman Zülch, *In Auschwitz vergast, bis heute verfolgt: zur Situation der Roma (Zigeuner) in Deutschland und Europa* (Reinbeck bei Hamburg: Rowohlt, 1979), 45.

31 Ibid., 48.

32 *The Romani-Jewish Alliance Newsletter* 1., from *Searchlight* (March 1995), and *The New York Times* (February 21, 1995.)

33 Tomasevic and Djuric, *Gypsies of the World*, 258.

34 Ibid., 258.

35 Ian Hancock, *The Pariah Syndrome* (Ann Arbor, Mich.: Karoma, 1987), 80, citing Henriette David, "Nouvelles de l'etranger: Allemagne," *Etudes Tsiganes*, 19 (1/2)): 75.

36 Tomasevic and Djuric, *Gypsies of the World*, 257–258.

37 Jack Anderson and Dale Van Atta, "West Germany Tries to Expel Its Gypsies," *The Washington Post* (December 24, 1989).

38 Serge Schmemann, "Gypsy Protesters Driven from a Nazi Camp," *The New York Times* (October 4, 1989).

39 Press release, SA-ROMA, P. O. Box 24051, Minneapolis, Minn. 55424, September 11, 1989, (Contact: Lois R. Duna).

40 Ibid.

41 Zülch, *In Auschwitz vergast*, 424.

42 Tomasevic and Djuric, *Gypsies of the World*, 260.

43 Press release, Romani Union, Manchaca, Texas, April, 1990.

44 "Gypsies say Holocaust Project Snubbing Them," *Dallas Times Herald* (June 28, 1984): A-23.

45 Hancock, *The Pariah Syndrome*, 80–81.

46 Ibid., 81.

47 Kenneth L. Woodward, "We Are Witnesses," *Newsweek* (April 26, 1993): 48.

EPILOGUE

1 Ian Hancock, *The Pariah Syndrome* (Ann Arbor, Mich.: Karoma, 1987), 112–113.

2 "Pueblo Authors Give Storytelling their Best," *The Pueblo Chieftain* (October 30, 1993): 5A.

3 William M. Kephart, *Extraordinary Groups, An Examination of Unconventional Lifestyles*, 3d ed. (New York: St. Martin's Press, 1987), 182.

4 Ian Hancock, "Gypsies: A People Forgotten," *The Humanist* (September/October 1985): 3.

5 Orrin Hatch, "An American Meditation on the Holocaust," *Reform Judaism*, 22, no. 2 (Winter 1993), 17.

6 "Forum," *National Geographic*, 186, no. 1 (July 1994).

Bibliography

༄

Acton, Thomas. *Gypsy Politics and Social Change: The Development of Ethnic Ideology and Pressure Politics among British Gypsies from Victorian Reformism to Romany Nationalism.* London: Routledge and Kegan Paul, 1974.

Ambrose, Stephen E. *Eisenhower: Soldier, General of the Army, President Elect, 1890–1952.* New York: Simon and Schuster, 1983.

———. *The Supreme Commander: The War Years of General Dwight D. Eisenhower.* Garden City, N.Y.: Doubleday, 1970.

Arad, Yitzhak. *Belsec, Sobibor, Treblinka: The Operation Reinhard Death Camps.* Bloomington: Indiana University Press, 1987.

Bar-On, Dan. *Legacy of Silence: Encounters with Children of the Third Reich.* Cambridge, Mass.: Harvard University Press, 1989.

Birkenfelder, Oskar. "Sinti und Roma im System der Totalerfassung," *Pogrom* (January 1983).

Blank, Rudolph, and Jurgen Roth. "Zigeunerlebel: Über ein Dasein zwischen Romantik und Wirklichkelt," from the German television program *Reportage am Montag* (ZDF), Fall 1985.

Blumenson, Martin. *Patton: The Man behind the Legend, 1885–1945.* New York: William Morrow, 1985.

Butler, Patrick. "Gypsies Claim They Are Getting a Bum Rap," *Booster* (May 3, 1989).

Cargas, Harry James. *Reflections of a Post-Auschwitz Christian.* Detroit: Wayne State University Press, 1989.

Chamberlin, Brewster, and Marcia Feldman, eds. *The Liberation of the Nazi Concentration Camps, 1945: Eyewitness Accounts of the Liberators.* Washington, D.C.: United States Holocaust Memorial Council, 1987.

Chicago Tribune (October 4, 1992): 18.

Clebert, Jean Paul. *The Gypsies.* Trans. Charles Duff. New York: Penguin, 1967.

Cohn, Werner. *The Gypsies.* Reading, Mass.: Addison-Wesley, 1973.

Conot, Robert E. *Justice at Nuremberg.* New York: Harper & Row, 1983.

Crowe, David, and John Kolsti. eds. *The Gypsies of Eastern Europe.* Armonk, N.Y.: M. E. Sharpe, 1991.

Dallas Times Herald (June 28, 1984).

Davis, Helen. "Angels of Life." *Hadassah Magazine,* November, 1985, 21–25.

Des Pres, Terrence. *The Survivor: An Anatomy of Life in the Death Camps.* New York: Oxford University Press, 1976.

Digest International (June/August 1988).

Diggs, J. Frank. *The Welcome Swede.* New York: Vantage Press, 1988.

Dobroszycki, Lucjan, ed. *The Chronicle of the Lodz Ghetto, 1941–1944.* Trans. Richard Lourie, et al. New Haven: Yale University Press, 1984.

Eiber, Ludwig. *Ich wusste es wird schlimm: die Verfolgung der Sinti und Roma in Munchen 1933–1945.* Munchen: Buchendorfer Verlag, 1993.

Eisenhower, Dwight D. *Letters to Mamie.* Ed. John S. D. Eisenhower. Garden City, N.Y.: Doubleday, 1978.

———. *The Papers of Dwight David Eisenhower.* Ed. Alfred D. CHandler, Jr. Baltimore: Johns Hopkins Press, 1970.

Ficowski, Jerzy. *The Gypsies in Poland: History and Customs.* Warsaw: Interpress Publishers, 1989.

———. *Gypsies on Polish Roads,* 3d ed. Krakow-Wroclaw: Wydawnictwo Literackie, 1985.

Frankl, Viktor E. *Man's Search for Meaning: An Introduction to Logotherapy.* New York: Simon and Schuster, 1984.

Friedman, Ina R. *The Other Victims: First-Person Stories of Non-Jews Persecuted by the Nazis.* Boston: Houghton Mifflin, 1990.

Friedman, Philip. "Nazi Extermination of the Gypsies." *Jewish Frontier,* January 1951.

Gilbert, Martin. *The Holocaust: A History of the Jews of Europe during the Second World War.* New York: Holt, Rhinehart and Winston, 1985.

Grynberg, Henryk. "Don't Universalize the Holocaust Memorial," *Midstream* (n.d).

Gutman, Israel, ed. *Encyclopedia of the Holocaust.* Vol. 2. New York: MacMillan, 1990.

Hancock, Ian. "The Eastern European Roots of Romani Nationalism." Paper presented at the Gypsy Panel, American Association for the Advancement of Slavic Studies, 20th National Convention, Honolulu, Nov 18–21, 1988.

———. "Fate of Hitler's Romani (Gypsy) victims yet to become part of Holocaust history." *The Detroit Jewish News*, n.d.

———. "Gypsies: A People Forgotten." *The Humanist* (September/October, 1985).

———. "Gypsy History in Germany and Neighboring Lands: A Chronology Leading to the Holocaust." Paper presented to the International Romani Union.

———. *The Pariah Syndrome: An Account of Gypsy Slavery and Persecution.* Ann Arbor, Mich.: Karoma Publishers, 1987.

———. "The Plight of the Romani Children." *Action for Children*, a publication of the NGO committee of UNICEF, vol. 2, no. 3, 1987.

Hart, Kitty. *Return to Auschwitz: The Remarkable Story of a Girl who Survived the Holocaust.* New York: Atheneum, 1982.

Hatch, Orrin. "An American Meditation on the Holocaust." *Reform Judaism* 22, no. 2 (Winter 1993): 16–17.

Heimler, Eugene. *Night of the Mist.* London: The Bodley Head, 1959.

Hilberg, Raul. *The Destruction of the European Jews.* Chicago: Quadrangle Books, 1961.

Hohmann, Joachim S. *Verfolgte ohne Heimat: Geschichte der Zigeuner in Deutschland.* Trans. Andrew Pollinger. Frankfurt am Main: Peter Lang, 1990.

Höss, Rudolph. *Death Dealer: The Memoirs of the SS Kommandant at Auschwitz.* Ed. Steven Paskuly. Buffalo, N.Y.: Prometheus Books, 1992.

Jazayery, Mohammad Ali, and Werner Winter, eds. *Languages and Culture: Studies in Honor of Edgar C. Polome.* Berlin: Mouton de Gruyter, 1988.

Die Judenfrage. Vertrauliche Beilage, April 15, 1942.

Kalisch, Shoshana, with Barbara Meister. *Yes, We Sang! Songs of the Ghettos and Concentration Camps.* New York: Harper & Row, 1985.

Katz, Steven T. "Gypsies under the Nazis." From a paper entitled "Quantity and Interpretation: Issues in the Comparative Historical Analysis of the Holocaust," n.d.

Kenedi, Janos. "Why is the Gypsy the Scapegoat and Not the Jew?" *East European Reporter* (1986).

Kenrick, Donald, and Grattan Puxon. *The Destiny of Europe's Gypsies.* London: Chatto-Heinemann for Sussex University Press, 1972.

———. *Sinti und Roma, die Vernichtung eines Volkes im NS-Staat.* Trans. Astrid Stegelmann. London: Chatto-Heinemann-Sussex, 1972.

Kephart, William M. *Extraordinary Groups: An Examination of Unconventional Lifestyles.* 3d ed. New York: St. Martin's Press, 1987.

Kogon, Eugen. *The Theory and Practice of Hell.* New York: Octagon Books, 1976.

Lebovitz, Shirley. *The Enduring Spirit.* Phoenix: Gildith Press, 1993.

Levi, Primo. *The Drowned and the Saved.* Trans. Raymond Rosenthal. New York: Summit Books, 1988.

Levin, Nora. *The Holocaust: The Destruction of European Jewry, 1933–1945.* New York: Schocken Books, 1990.

Liegeois, Jean-Pierre. *Gypsies: An Illustrated History.* Trans. Tony Berrett. London: Al Saqi, 1986.

Peter Lyon. *Eisenhower: Portrait of the Hero.* Boston: Little, Brown, 1974.

Maier, Charles S. *The Unmasterable Past: History, Holocaust, and German National Identity.* Cambridge, Mass.: Harvard University Press, 1988.

Mayer, Arno J. *Why Did the Heavens Not Darken? The Final Solution in History.* New York: Pantheon Books, 1988.

McDowell, Bart. *Gypsies: Wanderers of the World.* Washington D.C.: National Geographic Society, 1970.

Miller, Jim. "A War to Remember." *Newsweek* (September 4, 1989).

Milton, Sybil. "The Context of the Holocaust." *German Studies Review* 13, no. 2 (May 1990): 269–283.

Minneapolis Star and Tribune (March 25, 1986).

Muller-Hill, Benno. *Murderous Science: Elimination by Scientific Selection of Jews, Gypsies, and Others, Germany 1933–1945.* Trans. George R. Fraser. Oxford: Oxford University Press, 1988.

Necas, Ctibor. "Die tschechischen und slowakischen Roma im Dritten Reich." *Pogrom* (March/April 1981).

Newsletter of the North American Chapter of the Gypsy Lore Society (Summer 1982).

New York Times (March 14, 1988).

——— (October 4, 1989).

——— (February 14, 1990).

Novitch, Miriam. "Romani Genocide under the Nazi Regime." N.p. 1968.

Okely, Judith. *The Traveller Gypsies.* Cambridge: Cambridge University Press, 1983.

Paris, Edmond. *Genocide in Satellite Croatia, 1941–1945: A Record of Racial and Religious Persecutions and Massacres.* Trans. Lois Perkins. Chicago: American Institute for Balkan Affairs, 1961.

Persecuted and Forgotten. San Francisco: EBS Productions, n.d. Videotape in German with English subtitles and narration.

Puxon, Grattan. "Die Roma leben in Armut." *Pogrom* (March/April, 1981).

———. *See also* Kendrick, Donald.

Ramati, Alexander. *And the Violins Stopped Playing: A Story of the Gypsy Holocaust.* New York: Franklin Watts, 1986.

Ringelblum, Emmanuel. *Notes from the Warsaw Ghetto: The Journal of Emmanuel Ringelblum.* Ed. and trans. Jacob Sloan. New York: McGraw-Hill, 1958.

Ruzie, David. "Crimes Against Humanity: A New Approach After the Barbie Trial." *Justice* 2, no. 1 (Spring 1989).

SA-ROMA, Minneapolis, Minnesota. Press release, September 11, 1989.

Sijes, B. A. "Die Verfolgung der Roma in den besetzten Niederlanden 1940–1945." *Pogrom* (March/April 1981).

Starkie, Walter. *In Sara's Tents*. New York: E. P. Dutton, 1953.

Stojka, Karl. *The Story of Karl Stojka: A Childhood in Birkenau*. Washington, D.C.: United States Holocaust Memorial Council, 1992. Exhibition at the embassy of Austria, April 30 to May 29, 1992.

Tomasevic, Nebojsa Bato, and Rajko Djuric. *Gypsies of the World*. London: Flint River Press, 1988.

Trials of War Criminals before the Nürnberg Military Tribunals under Control Council Law 4, no. 10 (October 1946–April 1949). *The United States of America vs. Otto Ohlendorf*. Washington, D.C.: U.S. Government Printing Office.

Tritt, Rachel. *Struggling for Ethnic Identity: Czechoslovakia's Endangered Gypsies*. New York: Human Rights Watch, 1992.

Tyrnauer, Gabrielle. *Gypsies and the Holocaust: A Bibliography and Introductory Essay*. Montreal: Centre Interuniversitaire D'etudes Europeennes, 1989.

———. "'Uncle Mengele' Dispensed Candy, Death to Gypsy Children," *The Montreal Gazette* (June 15, 1985).

USA Today (February 9, 1990).

Vesey-Fitzgerald, Brian. *Gypsies of Britain: An Introduction to their History*. London: Chapman and Hale, 1944.

Washington Post (December 24, 1989).

Wiernik, Jacob. *A Yor in Treblinka*. New York: N.p., 1944.

Wiesel, Elie. Commemorative Address at the U.S. Holocaust Memorial Council in Memory of the Gypsy Victims of Nazi Genocide, Washington, D.C., September 16, 1986.

Wiesenthal, Simon. *Justice n'est pas vengeance: Une autobiographie*. Paris: Editions Robert Laffont, 1989.

Woodward, Kenneth L. "We Are Witnesses." *Newsweek* (April 26, 1993).

Wytwycky, Bodhan. "The Plight of the Gypsies." *The Other Holocaust: Many Circles of Hell*. Washington, D.C.: Novak Report on the New Ethnicity, 1980.

Yates, Dora E. "Hitler and the Gypsies." *Commentary* (November 1949).

Yoors, Jan. *The Gypsies*. New York: Simon and Schuster, 1967.

Zülch, Tilman, ed. *In Auschwitz vergast, bis heute verfolgt: zur Situation der Roma (Zigeuner) in Deutschland und Europa*. Reinbeck bei Hamburg: Rowohlt, 1979.

Index

℘

continued next page

continued next page

continued next column

continued next page

continued next page

About the Authors

BETTY ALT WAS BORN NOVEMBER 12, 1931, in Walsenburg, Colorado. She holds a B.A. in Sociology from Colorado College in Colorado Springs, Colorado, and earned her M.A. in History from Northeast Missouri State University in Kirksville, Missouri. Her publications include *Uncle Sam's Brides* (1990) and *Campfollowing: A History of the Military Wife* (1991). She presently teaches sociology at the University of Southern Colorado and the University of Colorado at Colorado Springs.

SILVIA FOLTS WAS BORN SEPTEMBER 18, 1953, in Krefeld, Germany, and came to the United States in 1979. She holds a B.A. in Organizational Communication from the University of Colorado at Colorado Springs and two M.A. degrees, one in Communication Theory from the University of Northern Colorado at Greeley, the other in Instructional Technology from the University of Colorado at Colorado Springs. She is presently the senior computer based training developer at Lam Research in Fremont, California.

Colophon

Design and typography by Tim Rolands
Cover and title page by Teresa Wheeler

Text and display set in ITC Legacy,
a Jenson revival designed by Ronald Arnholm

Printed and bound by Edwards Brothers, Ann Arbor, Michigan
Distributed by University Publishing Associates